The Most Beautiful Girl: A True Story of a Dad,
a Daughter and the Healing Power of Music:

Tamara Saviano's courageously written memoir *The Most Beautiful Girl* proves yet again that familial dysfunction is no match for the healing power of love and forgiveness. With Johnny Cash, Otis Redding and Charlie Rich providing, via the family turntable, the soundtrack to many a riveting scene, Tamara paints a picture of her early life in northern Wisconsin that is as harrowing as it is idyllic. This is the story of one heart's triumph over the human condition, told unflinchingly and without self-pity.

   —Rodney Crowell, author of *Chinaberry Sidewalks*

Tamara Saviano's journey from child of an alcoholic father to Grammy Award–winning record producer left me breathless. *The Most Beautiful Girl* is a triumph of the human spirit that resides in us all.

   —Marshall Chapman, author of *Goodbye Little Rock and*
   Roller and *They Came to Nashville*

The Most Beautiful Girl is Tamara Saviano's powerfully painful and beautifully written story of her transformation and redemption from dysfunctional childhood into a life filled with meaning, love and creativity. Driven by hard work, a passion for music and her ability to forgive and to move forward with her life, Tamara has emerged as one of the best friends Americana music has. But that's now. *The Most Beautiful Girl* is the story of how she became all she is.

   —Robert Hicks, author of *The Widow of the South*
   and *A Separate Country*

A courageous writer, Saviano explores a childhood that is bitter and wondrous, a place where madness and music mingle to tell us the truths about life.

   —Michael Streissguth, author of *Johnny Cash: The*
   Biography; Always Been There: Rosanne Cash, "The List,"
   and the Spirit of Southern Music; and *Like a Moth to*
   a Flame: The Jim Reeves Story

Tamara Saviano renders the truth of who she is with a gritty, unapologetic page-turner that will leave you captivated. Saviano's storytelling is skillful and refined, allowing her reader to trust and to be taken by the hand on this colorful journey of mind, body and most importantly—spirit. *The Most Beautiful Girl* is, in equal measure, excruciating and triumphant; ultimately delivering massive doses of compassion for those of whom she writes and for Saviano herself.
—Chely Wright, author of *Like Me: Confessions of a Heartland Country Singer*

In *The Most Beautiful Girl*, Tamara Saviano examines unmentionable scars and unthinkable sins with clear eyes and objective accountability. The author's singular style fortifies these vivid vignettes with authenticity that mirrors the legendary songwriters who sheltered her troubled youth. Saviano confronts demons directly. She seeks truths tirelessly. Her leanly crafted yet meticulously detailed prose proves undeniably: a truly fearless heart guides this remarkable journey toward salvation.
—Brian T. Atkinson, author of *I'll Be Here in the Morning: The Songwriting Legacy of Townes Van Zandt*

Music is the common thread that ties together so many of our life experiences, both good and bad. In *The Most Beautiful Girl*, Tamara Saviano brilliantly weaves together stories and songs to retrace the often painful but ultimately inspiring journey that has been her life so far. This unvarnished account of family dynamics is a riveting tale that readers will find both shocking and exhilarating.
—Dr. Gary Hartman, Director, Center for Texas Music History and author of *The History of Texas Music*

THE MOST
BEAUTIFUL GIRL

*A True Story of a Dad, a Daughter
and the Healing Power of Music*

TAMARA SAVIANO

Foreword by Kris Kristofferson

AMERICAN
ROOTS
PRESS

The Most Beautiful Girl: A True Story of a Dad, a Daughter
and the Healing Power of Music

Published in the United States of America by American Roots Press

FIRST EDITION
Book design by Barbara Aronica-Buck, www.bookdesigner.com
Front cover design by Shauna and Sarah Dodds, Backstage Design Studio, Austin, Texas
Copyeditors: Alanna Nash, Deborah Barnes, Catherine Fleming, Brian T. Atkinson,
  Jack Heffron and David Kessler
Proofreader: David Kessler

ISBN 978-0-9891243-0-0

For my first dad:
The late Robert Rae Ruditys Sr.
Aš myliu tave

I wished I could've stood
Where you would've been proud
That won't happen now
That won't happen now
        —Patty Griffin, from "Top of the World"

Hey, did you happen to see the most beautiful girl in the
  world?
And if you did, was she crying, crying?
Hey, if you happen to see the most beautiful girl that walked
  out on me
Tell her I'm sorry
Tell her I need my baby
Oh, won't you tell her that I love her
        —Charlie Rich, "The Most Beautiful Girl"

There's three sides to every story, Baby
There's yours and there's mine
And there's the cold hard truth
        —Don Henley, "Long Way Home"

FOREWORD

Tamara Saviano held up the Grammy she had just won. "Stephen Foster died a hundred and forty two years ago, and it's about time he got this," she said. And it was hard not to think that the words applied to her as well. The painful past revealed in her memoir bears little resemblance to the happily married, positive, creative person she is today.

Home was where the hurt was. At age 15—never an easy time of life—she discovered that the man she knew as her father wasn't, and the difficulties of their parent/teenager relationship understandably intensified. Alcohol didn't help. It's sad to see the attempts at a loving relationship (he taught her how to drive a car, forgave her when she wrecked his, got her a job and comforted her when she was fired the first day and got her another job, and bought her a car of her own) erased by physical and verbal abuse.

Her life turned around miraculously and this memoir is the story of that inspiring journey.

—Kris Kristofferson

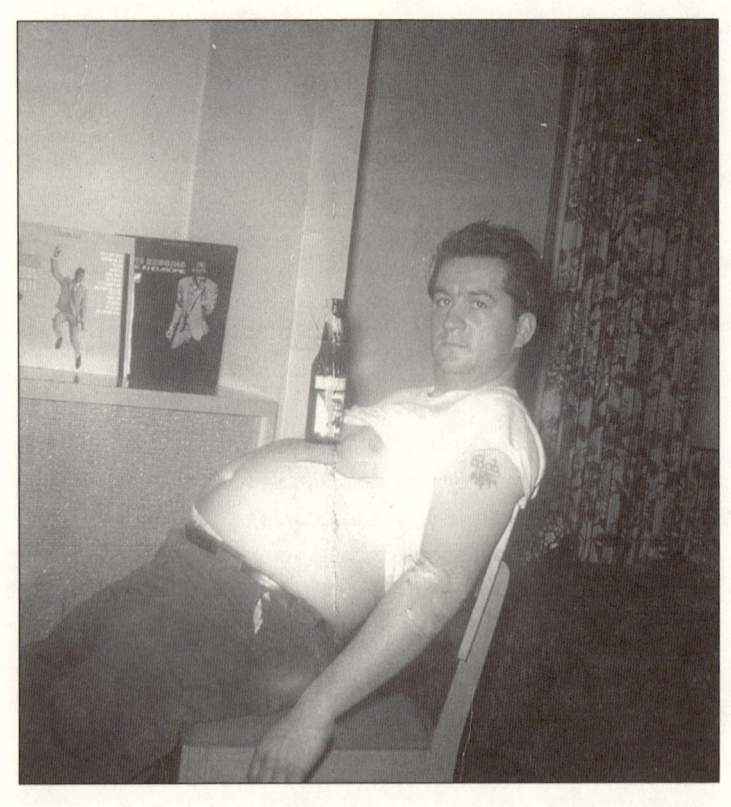

My dad, Bob Ruditys, with his Memphis Soul music collection. July 1968.

INTRODUCTION

This is a true story about my relationship with my first dad, Robert Rae Ruditys Sr., and how it shaped me. The events covered in this book are based on diaries I have kept since 1974, as well as interviews with people close to Dad and me, and extensive background research on my family history.

I have changed a few names to protect and respect my daughter's privacy. Aside from my daughter and her father, the names of the members of my family are accurate. My Mapleview friends are real people and I use their names. To simplify, the character of Kay is an amalgamation of several of my high school girlfriends.

I have made many mistakes in my lifetime. Like most people, I have regrets and sorrow, but I believe the path to happiness—and to wholeness—requires me to examine the past and come to terms with it. I hope this introspection will teach me to be more empathetic and open-minded. Like everyone else, I am still a work in progress.

I have no score to settle with my father, who died in 2001 after a full decade of not speaking to me. This is simply our story—a story that has deeply influenced nearly every aspect of my life. I came to realize how deeply during the research of this book. To my surprise, much of my success sprouted from coming to terms with this one relationship with my father.

If and when they read this, I hope my extended family will feel only compassion and love. I push forward with all due respect to their feelings.

—Tamara Saviano

PROLOGUE

School ends early on the last day of the semester and I'm pissed. This is not the way I imagined kicking off my fifteenth summer. I walk the six long blocks home, let myself into the house, and toss the tote bag with my locker contents into a corner. I place my report card on the kitchen table. My finger grazes over the ugly "D" in algebra that pulsates on the page like a heartbeat. I know there will be trouble. Dad won't care about the other marks—all he'll see is the big, fat "D."

Do I dare go to Kay's last-minute party? Mom and Dad are at work, so I decide to seize the few hours of freedom while I have the chance. I leave the report card on the table with a note that I'm at Kay's. I apologize for the bad grade and promise to study all summer. I'm not naïve enough to think I won't pay for this failure, but I try to push it to the back of mind for now. We leave tomorrow for Mapleview—our vacation home in northern Wisconsin—and this is my last chance to spend time with school friends until fall.

I'm happy at Kay's hanging out with my friends with *Frampton Comes Alive* on the turntable. Then I hear someone scream my name from outside and the voice echoes through the house: *Tammy! Tammy!* I lean over to turn the music down. It's Dad. My face burns with shame. I look around the circle on the floor and see pity in the eyes of my classmates. After nine years of school together, they know my dad.

He bursts down the stairs with Kay's mother. Prickly heat works its way from my core to my skin as Dad stomps over to me. He grabs my arm and pulls me up from the floor. I stumble as he jerks me up the stairs and out the door. As he hauls me toward the truck, Dad manages to slip his belt off to whip me. The leather strap stings my bottom and I plead for mercy.

"Please, Dad, stop. I'm sorry. I'll try harder. I won't get any more D's, I promise."

Dad ignores my cries. He continues to swing the belt fast and hard on my butt, back and legs. Red welts swell on my arms where I attempt to protect myself. Everything hurts. I drop to my knees, tilt my face to the sky and pray out loud. *Please, God, please give me strength.*

Dad's rage subsides and he lets go. He stares at me, his face twisted and vile, as I bow my head, clasp my hands together and whisper to God. Dad coughs. He wheezes and stumbles his way back to his truck and drives away.

• • •

We leave for Mapleview the next day. My brothers and I ride in the bed of Dad's pickup truck underneath a hard white canopy. Luggage is piled down the center and across the middle to form a cross. Each of us sits in a corner and I bounce around in my cramped little square trying to find a comfortable position. My entire body is bruised and battered. It's 80 degrees, but I'm wearing jeans and a long-sleeve shirt to cover the bruises on my back and arms and legs. My head still hurts and is covered with a blue bandanna. Big sunglasses hide my swollen eyes. Dad is especially nice to all of us. He's remorseful about beating me.

We stop at the Dairy Queen in Clintonville for ice cream. I think I'll throw up if I eat any, but I'm afraid to say anything. As we walk up to order, Dad throws his arm around my shoulder and sings the song:

> Hey, did you happen to see the most beautiful girl in the
> world,
> And if you did, was she crying, crying?
> Hey, if you happen to see the most beautiful girl who
> walked out on me,
> Tell her I'm sorry, tell her I need my baby.

• • •

He looks at me affectionately and the woman at the Dairy Queen window smiles. She thinks it's sweet that my dad sings to me.

"What do you want, El?" Dad asks.

"I'll just have a Coke." I can barely speak through the lump in my throat.

"What, no ice cream? You can have both if you want." Dad's brown eyes are moist with regret. They plead for forgiveness.

I give in. "Okay, I'll have a small vanilla cone, too. Thank you, Dad."

Mom and the boys rally around him to order ice cream. I walk over to a picnic table, lower myself gingerly on the bench and choke back tears. I ache all over yet I smile up at my father and hope I can hold it together for a few more hours.

When we arrive at Mapleview, I throw my suitcase on the bunk bed in the room I share with my brothers then run out the door and head into the freedom of the woods. I'm thankful that the tree house is empty. I feel every bruise stretch over sore muscles in my arms, legs and stomach as I climb the ladder. I reach the top and fall into the soft armchair, curl my legs into my chest and put my head down on my knees. Sweet relief. I cry for a long time, alone in the woods, camouflaged by the sound of the river washing by and the wind whistling through the pines.

THE MOST
BEAUTIFUL GIRL

Working with Kris Kristofferson at the Grand Ole Opry in 2003.

Johnny Cash Is Dead

I am at Johnny Cash's funeral. The pianist plays "I Walk the Line" as a haunting gospel hymn while the congregation settles into cushioned pews. The legendary singer's lifeless body lies in an open casket, dressed, of course, in black. The opening to Cash's 1970s television show flashes on an oversized video screen at the front of the church and we watch Johnny deliver his famous proclamation: "Hello, I'm Johnny Cash." He looks brutally handsome and dangerous and I half expect to see him walk out onstage with the Tennessee Three and kick off the show with "Folsom Prison Blues."

I pull my thin summer sweater around my shoulders. This moment feels like the real ending between Dad and me. I have a picture of my father, his black hair slicked back like the young Johnny Cash, leaning back in a chair and balancing a Pabst Blue Ribbon on his belly. His Memphis Soul album collection rests on a shelf next to him. Both my father and Johnny Cash were young and virile when the photo was taken in 1968. Now I'm at Johnny's funeral and Daddy is gone. He's only been dead for two years, but we were estranged for an entire decade before he died and time seems stretched thin. I haven't allowed myself to grieve either the demise of our relationship or Dad's death.

Johnny Cash has been entangled in my life from the time I was a small child, present mostly through his music, the ghost of a man I didn't really know. As a former music journalist and editor at *Country Music* magazine, I interviewed Johnny Cash a few times, but I'm here because of his relationship with my client Kris Kristofferson. I'm Kris's publicist, and today my job is simple: keep the media away. For Kris, this day is all about his friend John.

Kris's wife, Lisa, and their kids sit in the pew to my right. I'm on the aisle and try to collect myself as Kris paces back and forth to my left. He moves like a panther, slunk low, his shoulders hunched as he wears a path on the sea-green carpet. I focus on Kris's black trench coat as he circles. Reflections from the stained glass windows tinge his coat with shades of green and blue. Kris's agitation is contagious and I fold my hands together to stop them from shaking. I've been unsteady on my feet since an Associated Press reporter broke the news of Cash's death to me at six o'clock in the morning three days ago.

Al Gore stands at the altar behind a podium. As he eulogizes Johnny, Gore talks about how he was supposed to be the next president of the United States. He says if it were up to Cash, he would have been. The former vice president describes Johnny Cash as a man of contradiction—like Kris's song "The Pilgrim (Chapter 33)"—"a walking contradiction, partly truth and partly fiction"— and recalls how Cash faced his inner conflicts. He didn't deny or run from them. Instead, he embraced them as part of being human.

All of it reminds me of my own father. With each word, I sink deeper into my little corner of the church pew and try to make myself smaller and unnoticeable. It is surreal enough being here in the First Baptist Church, surrounded by people who knew and loved Cash without Dad's spirit fluttering around me. Tears flow down my cheeks but I am silent. I want to let loose and wail, but I contain myself. Although I am sad about Cash's death, it is the unfinished business with Dad that has its sharpened hooks in my flesh today.

I drift back to a time when I was five years old and my parents hosted a party in our basement rec room. I'm supposed to be asleep in my bedroom on the second floor, but instead I peer from behind the open basement door. I listen to the noises from below. Johnny Cash is on the stereo and his music drowns out the laughter and conversation between my parents and their friends. I duck my head back around the corner as I hear my dad's footsteps.

"I'm going to get some ice," he says.

"Bob, check on the kids while you're up there," Mom yells.

I hold my breath and tiptoe toward the stairs that lead to my room. I hear Daddy singing "Long Black Veil" as he pulls ice cube trays out of the freezer and cracks the metal handle to loosen the cubes. I'm almost to the stairs when he catches me.

"Penelope, what are you doing out of bed?" He calls me by my pet name.

"Couldn't sleep," I answer. I don't say that the music was too loud for anyone to sleep.

He picks me up. "C'mon, I'll take you back to bed. I inhale my father's Aqua Velva and brandy scent. Dad sings softly in my ear and carries me upstairs to the loft I share with my three brothers.

"She walks these hills in a long black veil, She visits my grave when the night winds wail," he sings. "Tomorrow I'll make pancakes when Mom's at work and we'll watch *Batman*, okay?" Dad leans over, kisses me goodnight and then moves around the room to check on my brothers.

My daydream becomes more vivid every minute. The next evening, while Mom works the night shift at the diner, Daddy puts

Johnny Cash on the turntable. My brothers and I dance around the living room with him. I've just started kindergarten and my brother Robbie's four. Stevie's two and Ricky just one. Our boxer puppy, Brandy, plays and twirls and barks and rolls and licks as Daddy takes turns lifting each of us off the ground to spin us. Of course, Daddy's singing:

> Hey, look a-yonder comin'
> Comin' down that railroad track
> It's the Orange Blossom Special
> Bringin' my baby back

Daddy drinks thirstily from his highball glass, the amber liquid only slightly diluted with a few ice cubes and a splash of soda. Robbie and Stevie make train whistle noises in their little boy sopranos while Daddy repeats the line "Well, I don't care if I do-die-do-die-do-die-do-die . . . " over and over and over again.

By suppertime, Daddy's voice sounds a little funny. His eyes droop and he stumbles as he rolls the television stand into the kitchen. He lifts Ricky into his high chair and settles the rest of us at the Formica table. I rub the chair's plastic-covered cushion to make it squeak. "Penelope, stop making that noise!" Daddy gives me the look, so I stop. "Turn on the TV and find *Batman*," he orders as he flips a pancake. We eat and watch *Batman. Pow! Wham! Holy bill of rights, Batman! To the Bat Cave, Robin!* And then we repeat that signoff we love to hear every time: *Same bat time, same bat channel!*

Ricky falls asleep in his high chair and his head bobs to one side. Stevie's face, sticky with maple syrup, is about to fall into his half-eaten pancake when Daddy scoops him from his chair. Daddy orders me to put the dishes in the sink as he lifts Ricky from the high chair with his free hand. Daddy holds one boy under each arm as he disappears around the corner and I hear his boots *click-clack* on the hardwood stairs to our bedroom. As he returns to get Robbie, I clear the table, careful not to drop any dishes.

"Okay, Penelope, time for bed," Daddy says after the boys are tucked in. "Go put on your pajamas and then come back down to give me a kiss goodnight."

I run upstairs to my bedroom. I change into my pajamas and creep back down the stairs and tip toe into the living room. The stereo is on and Daddy is singing with Johnny Cash again.

"Daddy?" I call. Johnny's drowning me out.

I try again. "Daddy?" I come up behind him in the living room as he gazes out the front picture window and watches dusk cover our small street. He jiggles the ice in his glass and continues to sing along with "Orange Blossom Special."

All of a sudden, he turns around and sees me. "Hey, I told you to go to bed."

"I came down to kiss you goodnight."

"Oh yeah." Dad crouches down to my level and opens his arms. I go to him and he kisses my cheek. He hugs me with the icy glass cold on my back.

"Goodnight, my Penelope."

I run back up the stairs, crawl into bed and pull my pillow over my head. It barely muffles Dad and Johnny Cash. They're singing like nobody's listening.

I swear I can smell that Aqua Velva and brandy at Johnny's funeral. My eyes pop open with the memory, but it's Kris's hand on my shoulder that truly jolts me back to today. I feel Johnny and my father in his fingertips, and I smile and nod to let Kris know I'm okay. He leans over me to kiss Lisa, and he walks to the front of the church to sing "Moment of Forever," a song he wrote when Lisa's father was dying. I lose the battle with my equilibrium as Kris sings, and when Emmylou Harris and Sheryl Crow follow him to harmonize on "The Old Rugged Cross," it all becomes too much. I hang my head and openly cry with the rest of the congregation.

Emmylou was around the last time I saw Johnny Cash. It was September a year ago when John and June and the rest of the remaining Carter Family performed for a small group at the Americana Music Conference in a ballroom at the Hilton Hotel in downtown Nashville. George Strait was across the street at the arena playing to a sold-out crowd of nearly twenty thousand, but the two hundred of us crowded into the small ballroom at the Hilton were together to witness history—John and June's last performance.

At the time, I was a producer for Great American Country (GAC) cable network, and we filmed the show. I interviewed Johnny and June later backstage after the show, and John looked tired and weathered and old. June was the spry one, yet she died first, eight months later, and most believe that June's death was the beginning of the end for John.

Rodney Crowell takes his turn at the podium, and recalls a conversation between his former wife, Rosanne Cash, and Johnny's mother Carrie. Rosanne had asked Carrie how she bore the pain of childbirth. "Child, we just endured it," was Carrie's response. Rodney relates that to how we will all have to live in a world without Johnny Cash: we will simply endure it.

My dad, Robert Rae Ruditys Sr., died suddenly of a heart attack on August 31, 2001. We hadn't spoken in a decade. I did make a few half-hearted attempts to reconcile, but truthfully, there was too much damage between us. I had somehow wiggled out of the chains that bound me to my family, and there was no way I was going back to that place.

Dad died the year I turned 40. Six years earlier I left my hometown of Milwaukee to work in the music business in Nashville. Leaving my old life behind and starting over was liberating and exhilarating. So much so that for a long time I pretended my old life didn't matter. Yet, today, memories of Dad are vivid, even more alive than they were at his funeral.

For much of my childhood my dad worked in a factory and moonlighted as an auto mechanic on nights and weekends. His greasy two-and-a-half-car garage was his favorite place. He wore blue coveralls and always had a wrench in one hand and a cocktail in the other. I often played on his big orange hydraulic jack while he worked. One day before he slid under the car, Daddy said: "Penelope, your eyes are especially blue today." He smiled up at me from the dolly and rolled himself under the car where he sang another Johnny Cash song:

No, I never got over those blue eyes
I see them ev'ry where

While Daddy sang to me from under the car, I hummed along and climbed on to one arm of the orange jack, pumped the handle to lift myself up in the air, then flipped the plastic hydraulic switch and rode back down to the ground. The air hissed around me under the sound of Dad's soulful voice. I did this over and over again until Dad slid out from under the car, yelled at me to quit playing with the jack and shooed me out of the garage.

Now Rosanne Cash is at the front of the congregation, remembering her father. "I can almost live with the idea of a world without Johnny Cash because in truth there will never *be* a world without him. His voice, his songs, the image of him with his guitar slung over his back, all that he said and sang and strummed changed us and moved us and is in our collective memory and is documented for future generations." Rosanne pauses before she continues. "I cannot, however, even begin to imagine a world without Daddy."

I flash back again, to my ninth Christmas morning. I sit cross-legged—rumpled and half-awake—next to my brothers in front of our Christmas tree. I stare at my pink flowered pajama bottoms as Mom cries and yells at Dad for ruining Christmas because he came home drunk late last night.

On Christmas Eve, my mother had fluttered about the house and wrung her hands, her eyes darting between the brightly wrapped gifts, tree lights twinkling and four eager kids waiting for the magic of Christmas to begin. There was no sign of Dad. Mom phoned every tavern in town looking for him while my brothers and I, dressed in our Sunday best, waited to eat Christmas Eve dinner. It was late when Mom kissed us and sent us to bed with promises of a Merry Christmas the next day. I awoke a little while later, not to the sound of Santa's reindeer, but to the crash of Daddy's Ford into the massive oak tree at the foot of our driveway. I crawled on my knees to peek out the window to watch Dad stumble through high snow banks on his way up to the house, lit only by the car headlights glowing through the falling snow.

On Christmas morning Dad's remorseful, at least until Mom pushes him too far. He sits in the gold velour chair in the corner next to the tree and hangs his head in shame as she stands over him and screams obscenities and threats. Mom leans over and pulls packages from beneath the tree, breaks them and hurls the wreckage at Daddy.

The partially wrapped cardboard sleeves from two LPs land at my feet, *Johnny Cash at Folsom Prison* and *Carryin' On* with Johnny Cash and June Carter. I pick up each of them, remove the rest of the red wrapping paper and smooth my hands over the covers. Jagged pieces of broken vinyl push against the inside of the cardboard. I wonder if I could glue the records back together. Maybe we would have a nice Christmas if Dad could listen to Johnny Cash.

Dad leaps from his chair and struggles with Mom. He screams at her: "Sandra, you need help. You're mentally ill. We need to have you committed."

He looks down at the four of us, still quiet in our places next to the sparkling Christmas tree. "See, kids, your mom is losing it. We're going to have to lock her up in a mental hospital."

Mom throws herself at Dad. "You bastard!"

Dad pushes her away, picks up the Christmas tree and heaves it across the room. My four-year-old brother Ricky, all white hair and fat cheeks, crawls into my lap, buries his head in my shoulder and cries. I try to comfort Ricky while Dad slaps Mom repeatedly as she begs, "Please, stop, the kids, it's Christmas."

"I hate fucking Christmas," Daddy yells as he shoves her to the ground and storms out the back door.

My brain is a time machine. As I sit in the church pew, it hop-scotches back and forth through the decades. Each painful memory bites me deeper. I relive the joyful moments with longing. I see myself as a young girl when my family took Sunday drives in the country. Dad led us in singing the Carter Family's "Church in the Wildwood" with his own version of the lyrics: "Oh come, come, come to the church in the wildwood, no lovelier church in the dale, no love is so dear to my childhood as the little brown church in the dale."

We sang that chorus over and over again—four kids shoulder to shoulder in the back seat of Dad's Ford. Mom would smile at Daddy from the passenger side, our dog Brandy curled at her feet. Sunday after Sunday, he drove us through the same Wisconsin country roads—blue sky and nothing but farm fields dotted with barns and old houses. Today, my heart aches for the family we were then.

Sorrow collapses upon me—a weight as heavy as this rigid church and the menacing solid wooden beams that hang above me. No one knows that I am weeping about my own father, wishing for a different ending to our story and knowing I'm never going to get it. Here I am, a middle-aged woman crying in a church far away from my family and still tormented by my dead father.

The Ruditys family in 1966. That's me in the middle, between Mom and Dad.

CHAPTER 2

He's a Problem When He's Stoned

As a child, I often laid back on my comforter in bed, hugged a feather pillow to my chest, pulled up the four corners to wrest the blanket around me and snuggled into the softness. I convinced myself I was safe—cocooned under God's watchful eye. In my young mind, He appeared as shadows and colors that remained so consistent I believed I was seeing a tangible incarnation. My faith in this spirit as my protector was unshakable.

Perhaps it's peculiar I had such faith. We were not a church-going family, and I had little religious training. It's possible my spirituality is born of the legends of my ancestors—kept alive by family stories passed down by my great-grandparents. Close proximity to the Catholics may have a hand in it.

Catholicism in all its forms is unavoidable in my hometown of St. Francis, Wisconsin—a blue-collar Milwaukee suburb on the southwestern shore of Lake Michigan. Religious institutions make up a full third of the three square miles of my hometown—an over-abundance of Catholic education. St. Francis is infamous for being the place where a Catholic priest, the Reverend Lawrence C. Murphy, molested more than 200 boys at St. John's School for the Deaf between 1950 and 1974. In 2010, the *New York Times* reported the scandal was covered up at the highest levels, most notably by Cardinal Joseph Ratzinger (a.k.a. Pope Benedict XVI).

Along with the Catholic churches, there is a smattering of Lutheran churches in the surrounding towns, and the tiny Cudahy United Methodist Church, where my grandparents worshipped. On the rare occasion I went to church, it was with my grandparents and the other Methodists.

Native Americans called my hometown *Nojoshing*, meaning "land that extends into the water," until my ancestors came along in the 1830s and renamed it Town of Lake. Not many years later the Catholics moved in. At the time, Town of Lake was bordered at the east by Lake Michigan stretching west to the town of Greenfield, north to Milwaukee's shipping bay and south to the city of Oak Creek.

Out of the township gradually evolved Bay View, Cudahy, and South Milwaukee and—after a hundred years of inhabiting the settlement along the western Lake Michigan shore—the Catholics finally convinced the local government to incorporate the City of St. Francis in 1951.

My mother's side of the family, none of them Catholic, inherited strong connections to the land and lake from our ancestors. My fourth great-grandfathers, George H. Wentworth and Jared Thompson, were among the first few settlers of Town of Lake. A few years after Indians "ceded" their land to the U.S. government in 1833, George Wentworth and his wife, Sylvia Packard, received 160 acres as a soldier's grant. George built his house and barn high on the hill overlooking Lake Michigan. In later years the property was known as Bessey's Hill because the Bessey family rented the house in the 40s and 50s. My mother and her friends sledded down Bessey's Hill each winter. Since 1962, my alma mater, St. Francis High School, has stood on that property. As a student there in the 1970s, I sat on the expansive green lawn that slopes down to Lake Drive and gazed out at the water as the strong lake wind blew my hair around my face. I closed my eyes and wished away the school and its modern arched façade and pretended that grandfather George's white clapboard farmhouse still stood behind me.

• • •

My earliest recollections are like a few faded Polaroid snapshots. The images are precious and visible, but time has aged the prints to fuzzy brown ghosts—Mom's tears falling on the ironing board as she presses a shirt and watches President Kennedy's funeral on TV; Grandpa holding me as a four-year-old to comfort me after I crack my head on Mom's headboard; Auntie Kathy taking my brothers and me out to trick or treat for Halloween; me gazing at my baby brother Rick through the bars of his crib that time we stayed with Auntie Donna when Mom was in the hospital for gallbladder surgery; and Daddy meeting me at the corner to walk me home from kindergarten. We swing our arms while we walk, my little hand folded gently into his rough palm. He gazes down at me and sings: "Oh Sweet Pea, c'mon and dance with me, c'mon c'mon, c'mon and dance with me. . . . Oh Sweet Pea, won't you be my girl, won't you, won't you, won't you be my girl?"

My most clear memories revolve around Dad. Day-Glo bright images of his larger-than-life personality dominate my childhood and young adult years while everyone and everything else are extras and stage props in the background of "our story." We even have our own soundtrack and still, when I hear those songs, picture-perfect visions of my dad dance through my brain the same way he shimmied his way through the house, singing along with his music.

Dad's nickname for me is Penelope Jones. No one remembers, if they ever knew, why he chose this pet name for me. Nobody else in my family refers to me as Penelope, and I like having a name that only my daddy calls me. Through the years he shortens Penelope to Elopee and by the time I reach high school he simply calls me El.

• • •

On Saturdays, I run errands with Dad. We usually go to Venus Ford so he can pick up auto parts and talk to his friends about deals on cars. I always wait patiently in the passenger seat and read my book while he's inside. Venus is on Packard Avenue—Cudahy's small main street lined with turn-of-the-century buildings that house local businesses, including the Hobby Shop, where we buy our 45 records, and Dutchland Dairy, which has the best shredded onion rings in town. I know if I'm good Dad will take me to both places.

True to his word, when Daddy finishes his work, we walk across the street to the Hobby Shop and head back to the racks of 45 records. He picks out a couple of records for himself and lets me choose my own. One morning I get the Archies' "Sugar, Sugar" and Tommy Roe's "Dizzy." Dad buys Rare Earth's "Get Ready" and Arthur Conley's "Sweet Soul Music."

We stop at Dutchland Dairy for a large order of shredded onion rings before we head for home. When we walk in the back door, Dad drops the onion rings on the kitchen counter as I run for the living room. The room is classic late 1960s décor: oversized gold velour couch with matching wraparound chairs, shag carpeting, dark paneled walls and a console stereo with an AM/FM radio, turntable and speakers built in to the wood cabinet.

"Penelope, wait for me!" he calls.

I carefully take "Sugar, Sugar" out of the paper sleeve and hand it to my dad when he walks in the room.

"Me first!" I shout.

"Okay, here, give me the record." My dad places the vinyl disc on the turntable and sets the needle to the beginning.

I dance around the room and sing with the chorus as those are the only lyrics I know. "Sugar, Sugar, ah honey, honey, you are my candy girl . . ."

Dad watches me, a playful smirk on his face. "You call that music?" He crinkles his nose.

He takes "Sugar, Sugar" from the turntable, puts "Sweet Soul Music" in its place and cranks the sound up loud as it will go. The picture window vibrates with the opening horns, and Dad moves his body to the beat. He bites his lower lip, bobs his head up and down, shakes his shoulders and rocks his hips as he makes his way to the kitchen to mix a drink. He returns seconds later, glass in hand, and sings:

Do you like good music
That sweet soul music . . .

Dad listens to the song once through and then drops the needle down in the middle of the song two more times to hear "spotlight on Otis Redding singing fa-fa-fa-fa-fa-fa-fa-fa . . . " He's playing the song for the fourth time when Mom comes into the room. Her dark hair is piled in a beehive that adds a good couple of inches to her tiny frame. Dad pulls Mom into his arms and holds her lightly, as if she is a delicate child. As they dance, he sings softly into her ear.

I sit on the floor and watch my parents. Mom's smile fades as Dad pulls away, drains his glass and heads to the kitchen for a refill.

• • •

I spend many Sunday mornings in my young life at Johnny's Lunch, the diner where my mom waits tables. The place is small with a few tables and a jukebox pushed against one wall. A long counter with stools runs on the side leading back to the kitchen where we can smell the bacon frying and hear the splatter of hot oil as pancake batter hits the griddle.

Our waitress, Ginny, is from the South and her drawl is downright musical compared to the hard consonant sounds of the German, Polish and Scandinavian immigrants in our town. Ginny refills Mom's and Dad's coffee cups often and lingers a few minutes to share local gossip. Dad flirts with Ginny and the other waitresses, and in return they tease him and make him laugh.

Regulars in the diner know my parents and stop over at our table to say hello. Sunday breakfast is a long, drawn-out social affair. Dad gives me dimes to play the jukebox. I love the colorful record sleeves on Hank Williams, Johnny Cash, Lynn Anderson, Elvis Presley and Ray Price records perched above the sparkling mirrors of contact paper that cover the front of the player. It soothes me to hear Hank Williams drawl "Hey Good Lookin'" and Lynn Anderson sing "Rose Garden" as I watch my parents mingle with the other diners.

Our Sunday routine is different in the fall. Mornings are devoted to preparing to watch Green Bay Packer games on television. Dad and I run to the liquor store in the morning to buy hot ham and rolls (a Sunday tradition in Wisconsin) and then to Grebe's Bakery for donuts—jelly-filled for Dad, chocolate custard for Mom, long johns for the boys and a cruller or peanut square for me. We eat donuts for breakfast and ham sandwiches during the Packer game. I wear my Bart Starr T-shirt during the game although secretly Donny Anderson is my favorite Packer because he is the cutest one. Dad sits on the couch and yells at the television during the game. During his quieter moments, he reaches down where I sit on the floor leaning against his legs and massages my head. Most of the time, this lulls me into a soft slumber until Dad screams at the TV again. During halftime, Mom shoos me upstairs to take a nap.

I spend the rest of Sunday afternoons reading my Trixie Belden books. I'm a shy girl and my best friends are the books' fictional characters: Trixie and her gang of Bobwhites. My parents worry about the amount of time I spend with my "nose in a book" as Dad says. Almost every day Mom tells me to go outside and get some fresh air, but I prefer reading in the safety of my room, where I can hear Daddy through the floorboards as he sings along with his music.

When I do go outside, it's usually to the platform Dad built for me in the cherry tree outside our kitchen window. I wedge my foot into the low V of the tree trunk, pull myself up and use the thick low-hanging branches as steps to the plywood floor hidden in the leafiest part of the tree. I sit there for hours at a time and play my transistor radio, read books and talk to my Barbie dolls.

I'm surrounded by my safe, small world in the tree—our back yard lined with blackberry bushes, rhubarb plants and the white smelly peonies; Dad's garage and the comforting clink of his tools and warmth of his vocals as he sings; the shrieks of my brothers as they play football in our oversized front yard; and Mom keeping an eye on me through the window as she works in the kitchen.

• • •

Dad makes extra money in the winter by hooking a plow to the front of his truck so he can clear snow out of parking lots, driveways and alleys. I ride with him some mornings. Dad kneels at the side of my bed before daylight and whispers in my ear to get up quietly. He doesn't want me to wake Mom and the boys. I dress and tiptoe down to the kitchen where Dad fills two Thermos canisters—

coffee for him and hot chocolate for me. After he plows our drive-way, Dad heads straight over to Grandma and Grandpa's and cleans the alley behind their garage. Grandpa will need to get his car out to go to work. As he plows, Dad keeps the radio tuned to my favorite radio station, WOKY, and we listen to music together.

After he clears the way for Grandpa, Dad drives around town to see who else needs help digging out of the snow. Although folks slip him fives and tens, I believe my dad likes to do his small part to ease the cold Wisconsin winters.

It's Dad's contradictions that confuse me as a child. His soft spot is as vast and wide as his mean streak. Many people that know my dad adore him. Sometimes when he is drinking, and mostly when he's not, Dad is a lot of fun. He is gregarious and always, always the life of all parties, many of which he hosts. When sober, Dad is openhearted, kind and generous. I've heard his friends say many, many times: "Bob Ruditys would give the shirt off his back to help a friend."

Those friends don't see the other side. When he's drinking, Dad's cruelty to his family knows no bounds. It seems there is a relentless battle between good and evil raging deep inside him. When Dad is dead drunk, he is explosive. He screams. He spits obscenities and throws glasses and dishes around the house. Some-times he smacks the walls and other times he hits us. At times, he is so scary that I truly believe he might murder all of us one day. Any-thing can set him off and I live in fear of making him angry. In this frame of mind, Dad calls himself "The King." "Don't fuck with The King," he'll snarl, "because you will lose."

From one day to the next, I struggle to judge his moods, to understand his fascination with liquor, and to figure out what I can do to keep him happy. My mom, brothers and I all stiffen when Dad walks in the room. We're like dogs: We cower with our tails tucked under when Dad is angry. We wag and drool and jump when he's happy.

My father was raised in St. Francis. He was the youngest of Joseph and Elizabeth Ruditys' four children. From his accounts, it seems that Dad was at best ignored by his parents and at worst abused by them. Joe and Liz were notorious "juice bags," and spent every night, including holidays, drinking at Al & Angie's tavern, Iowa Tap or Kansas Bar. Elizabeth was especially distant and cold to her youngest son. She didn't cook dinner for him, or check his schoolwork, or take him to the doctor or make sure he had appropriate clothing for school.

The Ruditys family immigrated to St. Francis by way of Michigan's Upper Peninsula, probably around the 1920s. At the turn of the century, social workers sometimes complained that drinking was the one serious vice of Eastern European working-class immigrants, since it often brought physical and financial hardship. Had I been studying this phenomenon, I would have used the Ruditys clan— of Lithuanian descent—as a prime example of this criticism. They are—and seemingly always have been—a hard-drinking, hard-fighting, and hard-living people.

In St. Francis and the surrounding communities, the Ruditys boys were reputed to be law-breaking troublemakers and even into my generation the notoriety is well earned with two of my brothers and my cousins. Partly because of congenital heart problems and partly because of lifestyle, the Ruditys men rarely live to see age 60.

My dad learned to fend for himself at a young age. He and his siblings were paid an allowance to keep the house clean and even on the prettiest summer days, Dad scrubbed kitchen floors on his hands and knees, vacuumed the carpet, washed dishes and laundry, and listened to R&B music in the background. Dad remained a compulsive housecleaner throughout his life.

As a teenager, my dad spent his time with music and cars. He held jobs at several gas and service stations and often rebuilt and repaired engines at home. Dad and his buddies frittered away many hours in the Ruditys' yard washing and polishing Dad's cars.

Without parental guidance, there was no one to influence Dad to stay in school and he dropped out before he finished high school. There is no doubt my dad was a hell-raiser. By the time he was in his early teens, Dad and his friends brewed dandelion wine in the Ruditys' family basement and broke into houses to steal liquor. When he was 14, Dad had to have his stomach pumped from drinking so much.

Perhaps because he was so neglected by his parents, I learn early on that my dad is possessive with friends—male and female. He wants attention and control. As a young man, when Dad dated, he was consumed by that need. He'd fixate on his girl and wonder out loud where she might be and with whom. To the surprise of his tough pals, my dad wanted to "go steady" rather than play the field. I think because he lacked a caring family, Dad was hungry for affection and tried to surround himself with people who provided him with unconditional love and loyalty.

As I mature, I believe Dad is afraid of intimacy because it opens him up to the possibility of pain. Dad is thin-skinned and easily hurt. He strikes back when he is angry and never gives in or accepts an apology after a certain line is crossed and he feels betrayed.

My dad wants everyone to fit the image he has created in his own mind. He doesn't want people to disappoint him as he's had enough disappointment in his own family. He learns to hold a grudge at a young age.

There are times in my life when my dad is my staunchest ally and strongest supporter. There are other times when he crushes me like an empty can of Pabst and tosses me away like last week's trash.

I've witnessed Dad cut several people out of his life. Never, not even for a moment, did I consider I'd be one of them.

I was wrong.

• • •

At age 10, my favorite car is the Corvette. I point them out on the road and in car magazines and brag to anyone who listens that someday I am going to have my own purple 'Vette. One afternoon I hear Dad pull up the driveway shouting, "Hey Penelope, come out here!"

I run outside. Dad stands next to a gorgeous purple Corvette convertible he borrowed from a friend. I throw myself into his arms. "Oh Daddy! A purple 'Vette!" He grins. "C'mon Penelope, let's go for a ride."

I buckle myself into the low passenger seat as Daddy backs down the asphalt driveway. He turns out carefully, winks at me, throws the car in gear and burns rubber. I squeal in horrified delight. As we head north on Lake Drive, Dad tunes the radio to our favorite station. As Janis Joplin sings "Me and Bobby McGee," Daddy takes his eyes from the road for a second to smile at me as he turns up the volume. He turns his eyes back to the road and mimics Janis Joplin's growl:

Freedom's just another word for nothing left to lose,
Nothing don't mean nothing if it ain't free

Daddy sings the song to me word-for-word, his eyes veering from the road now and then to smile at me. We continue on Lake Drive north of the city past the McKinley Marina, Bradford Beach and Lake Park, through Shorewood, Whitefish Bay, Bayside and Grafton. Daddy's got his window down, the crook of his left arm on the door. He wears his standard white Fruit of the Loom T-shirt with the sleeves rolled up. A heart-shaped tattoo stretches across his broad bicep. The tattoo used to read "Carolyn," but Mom made him fill it in when they got married and now the heart is filled with green and red swirls. My dad's silky black hair blows in the wind; pork chop sideburns scratch the side of his face. His barrel-shaped chest is close to the steering wheel and his legs are so short he seems to stretch unnaturally for the gas pedal. It is unseasonably warm and people flock to the lakefront and beach, all white skinny legs and pale faces yearning for sunlight after a long Wisconsin winter.

We return to our south side of town, drive down Wentworth Avenue and turn east on Estes Street to get to South Shore Park. Many street names and landmarks around this area are named for my ancestors and they are constant reminders of our family legacy. The connection is particularly strong as I roam the land where the family estate once stood and the adjacent Lake Michigan frontage so dear to me.

When my fourth great-grandfather George Wentworth died here on December 23, 1901, at age 86, he was saluted as "the man who had lived in Milwaukee longer than any man now living." George lived long enough to meet his great-granddaughter, Myrtle Gertrude Thompson, who was three years old when he died. Gertie is my great-grandmother and she is a vital force in my life until she dies in 1990. In my mind, because George loved Gertie and Gertie loves me, there is only one degree of separation between George and me.

Gertie's other great-grandfather, Jared Thompson, was elected the first chairman of Town of Lake in April 1842. He owned a tin store on Water Street and was a member of the county board of supervisors, a justice of the peace and a local Methodist minister. Around 1865 Jared deeded his land to the school district to build a school. Thompson Avenue Elementary School is still in operation during my childhood, and many of my friends attend school there. Jared died at the age of 85 in 1890.

My great-grandmother Gertie is a Wentworth by her mother and a Thompson by her father. The Wentworths and Thompsons are strong stock. Even in the 1700s and 1800s, many of them lived more than 80 years. More recent generations have lived into their 90s and longer.

During the first 30 years of my life I am surrounded with four—sometimes five—generations of my family living within a few miles. It seems perfectly ordinary to me that I have grandparents and great-grandparents as a part of my daily life.

Dad and I drive up and down the lakefront streets showing off the borrowed Corvette for several hours. We're both in a good mood when we return from cruising. Daddy fixes himself a drink and puts on some music. As he gets drunk on brandy and soda cocktails, the music gets louder. When Dad gets like this, it doesn't matter if it's a school night or that any of us are studying or sleeping.

He'll typically latch onto a few songs he wants to hear over and over again. Otis Redding's "Sittin' on the Dock of the Bay," Wilson Pickett's "Midnight Hour," Aretha Franklin's "Respect," Charley Pride's "Kiss an Angel Good Morning," Johnny Rivers's "Brown Eyed Handsome Man" or anything by Johnny Cash.

Even in a drunken stupor, my father can place the record player needle exactly in the right groove of an LP to replay the same line in a song over and over again. Tonight he sings along in a country-western twang to Cash, as he lowers the needle again and again on the same lyric: "I shot a man in Reno, just to watch him die."

That's me on the left with my friends Debbie and Janette Hoppe on the pier at Mapleview in 1970.

CHAPTER 3

Girl From the North Country

Along with my grandparents, one of the saving graces of my childhood is life at Mapleview Resort. I feel the purest happiness there. My family begins vacationing at Mapleview in 1969 when Dad's friends Jerry and Izzy Osiecki buy the resort.

Mapleview is really more like a camp. It's definitely not the upscale luxury people usually think of when they hear the word "resort." Mapleview is a quintessential northern Wisconsin kind of place—a campground on a rural lake with some cottages and a lodge. We are working-class families from Milwaukee and Chicago who drive a few hundred miles "up north" to get away from life in the city.

Mapleview is deep in the Northwoods of Wisconsin in the town of Conover, about 11 miles north of Eagle River (Snowmobile Capital of the World), and is less than 10 miles south of Michigan's Upper Peninsula. Vilas County holds nearly 55,000 acres of the Nicolet National Forest. A satellite image of the region shows the towering old growth woodland in a rough, sprawling green scattered with crystal-clear lakes that are absolutely mystical to me. In all the places I've traveled since, nothing has ever come close to matching the beauty of northern Wisconsin.

The Osiecki family lives on the second floor of the lodge—the rustic centerpiece of our community. The lodge is a bar and restaurant, and it's the daily meeting place for the families who vacation at Mapleview. The windows in front of the bar look out over the 427 acres of Pioneer Lake, which anchors one side of the property.

Mounted fish and stuffed deer, and other animals fill the pine-paneled walls. Bar signs reading "Next Time Bring Your Wife," "Don't Just Sit There Nag Your Husband," and "Oshitski's Polish Retreat" hang randomly among the dead game.

Pine needles cover snowmobile and hiking trails that weave through the 80 acres of woods in and around the boundaries of Mapleview. Small 1940s-era cottages, nestled in small groves of white and jack pine, line up on either side of the lodge. A dirt road leads back to the campground next to Pioneer Creek. The creek forms the southern border of the resort and feeds into heart-shaped Pioneer Lake. A row of permanent mobile homes parallels the creek and guards the campground like soldiers on night watch.

Each trailer home has a small yard with a campfire pit surrounded by benches and lawn chairs. Some of the families decorate their yards with colored lights and hummingbird feeders. Driftwood signs carved with the family names mark each trailer: LEE, BOGATZKE, BEYER, RUDITYS, KAYSER, BARTEL, MOLTER.

Not including the Osieckis, 34 of us live in permanent trailers in the back of the campground. We're seven sets of parents and 20 kids, and the resort culture forms intimate ties between our families. Rituals mark the years: the snowmobile derby in January, winter frolics in February, opening fishing weekend in March and preparing the trailers for summer in April, Memorial Day weekend, potluck dinners, Fourth of July, musky bakes in the campground, the Vilas County Fair in August, Labor Day chicken barbecues, the autumn color festivals and pig roasts in October, deer hunting and

Thanksgiving, Christmas, snowmobile trail rides and celebrating each New Year's Eve with a big bash at the lodge.

Growing up at Mapleview is like a decade-long coming-of-age film. My friends and I run around the resort blissfully neglected by our parents. This is their vacation and chance to get away from work and the pressures of running the household. They know we are safe at the resort and we follow one simple rule: we aren't allowed to leave the property without permission. This leaves plenty of choices. The summer is long, Mapleview is our playground, and our parents are small annoyances.

With the exception of a few little ones, we kids fall into an age spread of about 10 years. Our crowd is Jerry Jr. ("Little Jerry") and Tony Osiecki; Kathy, Donna and Bobby Lee; Denise and Paula Beyer; Annette and Jeanette Bogatzke; Bobby and Patty Kayser; Mary and Doug Molter; my brothers and me. During the summer months, Mapleview rents out weekly campsites and we have summer friendships with the Mudler boys (Mike, Mark, Dan), Steve, Dave and Peggy Murray, the Michalkiewicz family (Missy, Tammy, Rocky), the Strong sisters (Sherry and Barb), Chuck Carrington, Eugene Lang, Phyllis Moffat. Other boys and girls just float in and out of our lives.

Even all these years later time stands still at Mapleview. The sounds, sights and smells take me back to my youth: wind as it rushes through the trees; gentle ripples that move across the lake; the smell of campfire mixed with balsam, cedar, spruce and pine; the purple wash of the northern lights across the sky; and the dome of stars that hover protectively over the resort.

A memory hangs around every corner—the spot in the campground where I watch Little Jerry gut a deer; the swarm of bees that chase my brother Steve into the lake; our gang winning the grease pole competition every year at the Vilas County Fair; playing foosball and listening to the jukebox in the game room; we rake huge leave piles to jump into each fall; Mom skis behind the boat in a snow-mobile sled; Dougie chases me with the snowmobile; my dad chews on a beef jerky with a drink in front of him at the bar; we shine flashlights and look for bear at the dump; Mary stands on a picnic table and sings; we eat Izzy burgers at the lodge; we ride our bikes off the end of the pier and crash into the water; the musky bakes in the campground; Dad stands in the lake while he is drunk and sings "He Turned the Water into Wine," snowmobile trail rides to Bauer's Dam and Burnt Bridge and winter picnics at the park; Mary cro-chets beer can hats; Mr. Kayser and Mr. Lee catch humongous muskies; the "band" plays homemade instruments and everyone dances to the music made by the stump fiddle and garbage-can bass; fireworks over the lake; the Chain Skimmers water ski show in town; and the image of myself as a teenager as I walk barefoot in cut-off shorts over my swimsuit, a dimpled bottle of Fresca in my hand and Noxzeema tingling on my forehead.

We spend winter hours in Izzy's kitchen and play the flour game: Pack flour into a measuring cup, dump it upside down on a plate and place a nickel on top of the mold. We each take a turn slicing wedges of the packed flour with a butter knife around the coin. Whoever makes the nickel fall has to eat what the other kids can fit onto one teaspoon. The loser stomachs concoctions of mus-tard, horseradish, butter, ketchup, bacon grease and all the other gross things we can find in Izzy's refrigerator.

We pile into the ladies' room in the lodge, turn off the light, stare into the mirror and chant, "I believe in Mary Worth" three times to conjure up the urban legend ghost. More than once, Izzy reaches in the door, flips on the light and scares the heck out of us.

"You kids quit playing in the bathroom," she yells as we scream past her, our hearts pound as if we really did see Mary Worth in the mirror.

We make fun of the regular customers in the lodge, particularly the locals. Our favorite target is Iris Brown. She's a sweet old lady, but we pick on her distinct way of smoking a cigarette. Iris curls her lower lip around the filter and makes a loud sucking noise as she inhales and exhales and Dougie perfects his impression and we egg him on to do it again and again.

We sneak into the outdoor theater and sit on blankets on the ground in the dirt field, surrounded by looming pines and squawky metal speaker boxes. Spilled Pabst and popcorn smells fill the air as we drink the beer and booze the boys ripped off from McKeever's grocery. We laugh amid the glow of cigarettes and joints being passed in front of the animated dancing hot dog.

I still hear the echo of us singing the John Denver hit "Take Me Home Country Roads" by the campfire in front of the lodge. I see the ghost of my dad holding court in the lodge as he laughs at his own favorite joke and holds his heart and bellows: "I'm having the big one, Sandy . . . this is the big one!"

Everyone owns boats and we ski, fish and paddle canoes around the lake and creek. When we aren't on the water, we spend our time in the barn, which is the game room with a jukebox, foosball tables and pinball machines, or at the tree house the boys built in the woods near the river. The tree house is a rough two-story structure built about 20 feet off the ground. Scrap pieces of two-by-fours are nailed into the tree as a stepladder. The tree house floor and walls are constructed from the wood from pine trees.

The tree house is lavish for a house built by a group of teenagers. The first floor is covered with a spare scrap of orange and white shag carpet from my bedroom in St. Francis. I'm not there to witness it, but somehow the boys manage to get an old battered recliner and a double-size mattress up the ladder. The mattress is sprawled on the roof and is damp and bug-infested. But the recliner is comfortable and sheltered from weather. If our parents know the tree house exists, they don't know exactly where it is and certainly never come to check it out.

Our parents seem to have complete trust in Little Jerry, who really isn't little at all. He is the oldest Osiecki son and a bit older than the rest of us. One summer day when he's 16, Jerry saves three lives in one day. In the morning, he rescues two fishermen from drowning after their boat capsizes. Later that day, Jerry rushes a heart attack victim to the hospital rather than wait for an ambulance to drive all the way in from Eagle River. The local newspaper sends a reporter and photographer out to Mapleview and publishes a spread about Jerry's heroism. It's no wonder we look up to him.

Jerry owns a 1942 Willys Army Jeep and is driving it by the time he's 13. Although designed to seat four, it doesn't have a top and, if we sit on each other, we can cram six to eight kids into the Jeep. Jerry zooms through the trails in the woods and leads us in song: "Everything's made for a Jeep!" Jerry sings. We're his chorus and shriek in unison: "A Jeep!" We sing back and forth as we speed through the forest, wind in our hair, sun dappling the tree trunks, mud splashing beneath the tires. Happy kids bump up and down in the Jeep bed.

Mary Molter is my best friend at Mapleview. Mary is the closest thing to a sister I have during my childhood. We are geeky girls— caterpillars hoping to one day emerge as butterflies. Dad adores Mary. She isn't as serious as me, and when Dad teases her, she gives it right back to him and always knows what to say to make him laugh.

Mary teases Dad by flicking her retainer down with her tongue to reveal the soft pink plastic piece that fits in the top of her mouth. For some reason, Dad is completely grossed out by it.

"Mary, please stop!" He shudders dramatically and laughs at her.

It makes Mary giggle to see his reaction and she flicks her retainer up and down each time he enters the room. When Mary grows out of her retainer, she wraps it up and presents it to Dad as a birthday gift.

Mary accepts my dad the way he is. She knows he has issues with alcohol and that his temper gets out of control, but Mary shrugs it off as part of the culture we live in. The people of Wisconsin love to drink and Dad is not unusual.

• • •

Once we discover Mapleview, our family life at home in St. Francis becomes secondary. We spend weekends, holidays and summers at Mapleview. Every extra dollar Mom and Dad earn is for the sole purpose of spending more time at the resort. Mom works overtime at her new factory job at EZ Paintr for extra gas money and a fund to eat and drink at the lodge. Dad takes on extra freelance mechanic work so he can afford to buy a boat and snowmobiles and outdoor gear. I have friends at school, but my primary focus is life at Mapleview. When I want to learn to play the drums in junior high, Dad talks me out of it and buys me a snowmobile instead. Band practice would take time away from Mapleview. I'm easily persuaded. Even when I am home in St. Francis, I spend hours writing long letters to Mary, Bobby and Patty Kayser and Mark Mudler. These are the friends I tell all my hopes and dreams.

At Mapleview, Dad tries hard to give us the kind of experience he didn't have as a child. He dives into the lifestyle wholeheartedly to make it fun for our entire family. We have a ski boat and he spends hours pulling us and the other kids behind it. Dad builds a big fire pit in our yard and buys a gleaming set of four pudgy pie makers. Mom stocks the kitchen with white bread and fillings for our pudgy pies—ham, cheese, cherry and blueberry pie filling. Dad fashions long metal skewers especially for roasting marshmallows over the fire to make s'mores. And he stocks up on copper tubing, cuts it to length and fits the pieces inside green rubber garden hose. We throw these chunks into the fire to make it burn blue, purple and green flames.

Dad buys into the citizen-band radio craze and we have a portable CB in the car and a base at the trailer. Dad's handle is "The Dealer" and Mom is "The Dealer's Wife." On the way to Mapleview, Dad checks in with the other families on the CB. "Breaker 1-9 this is The Dealer. Hey Smoke Eater, you got your ears on? What's your twenty?"

Mr. Kayser, a firefighter, is "Smoke Eater" and Mrs. Kayser is "Amazing Grace." The Kaysers live in Chicago and are behind us on the road many times as Dad talks them through the maze of state troopers on the highway.

"I'm in the hammer lane and got your front door covered here, good buddy," Dad says. "There's a bear in a plain brown wrapper just south of Butte des Morts."

• • •

One winter day when I'm 12, my friends and I sled down the hill next to the bunkhouse. It's a perfect path, the snow packed down by the weight of snowmobiles that run across it. A thin layer of ice crusts the snow and gives our sleds more speed. The hill leads down to the parking lot next to the lodge. It's dark at the top of the hill in the woods and only faint, fuzzy light shimmers from two street lamps at the bottom of the hill and the distant lamps in the lodge window.

We take turns sledding down the hill on a saucer until Little Jerry walks up the hill, a rectangle of polished Formica under his arm.

"Hey you guys, try sledding on this—it'll really fly."

Jerry hands the Formica to his brother Tony, who immediately drops to the ground and pushes himself off.

"Wahhhhhhh, Wowwwwwww!" Tony screams as he zooms down the hill.

We can't see him at the bottom. Doug is ready to take off on the saucer and the other boys are situating themselves on the toboggan when Tony huffs back up to the top of the hill.

"You gotta try this, it's really fast." Tony hands the Formica to Doug.

Everyone takes turns with the Formica.

"I want to try it," I say as Bobby Lee walks back up the path after his turn. He hands me the Formica. I set it down and carefully climb on, cross my legs and grip the sides with each mittened hand. Bobby gives me a friendly push.

I barrel down the path and scream gleefully. Trees whiz by in the shadows and snow dust flies in my face. Halfway down the Formica spins around and I fly down the hill backward. It's dark and I can't see my friends, but I hear the faint sound of their voices. I think they are cheering me on. I yell louder. The Formica spins again, and SMACK! Pain and darkness engulf me. I pass out cold.

As I drift back to reality, I try to get up but something heavy pins me down. I scream and cry: "Tony! Tony, get me out of here! Help, Tony!" I don't know why I yell for Tony, but his is the only name that comes to mind.

"I'm here." Tony's voice sneaks in from the left as he yanks my parka. At some point, I realize Tony is pulling me out from under a pick up truck. I reach up to touch my aching forehead. Something warm runs in my eyes and my mitten comes away wet and sticky.

Tony helps me to my feet but my knees give out. He picks me up to carry me. We're the same size and Tony struggles to hold me draped across his arms. My head throbs and I feel faint.

"Oh my God!" Tony shrieks when he sees my face. He carries me to the lodge. He stands on the porch and struggles to keep me in his arms as he kicks the lodge door.

"Someone let us in! Open the door!" Tony yells. I black out.

When I come to, we are in the lodge kitchen. I'm slumped on a chair as Izzy Osiecki kneels in front of me and presses a white towel to my forehead. As she brings each towel away from my head, it is stained red with my blood. Out of the corner of my eye, I see Tony pull my mom into the kitchen. Her eyes widen when she sees me.

"Oh my God, what happened? What happened?" My mother is frantic.

"We were sledding and she hit a parked truck," Tony answers.

"Oh my God, there's so much blood," Mom says.

"Sandy, head wounds bleed a lot," Izzy says. She remains calm and continues to hold a towel on my head. "Someone take Tammy to the hospital. I think she needs stitches."

I pass out again at "stitches." When I come to, I see headlights coming toward me on a dark road. I jump.

"It's okay, Penelope." Daddy's arm is around me and I'm pressed between him and Mom in the front seat of the car. Daddy drives with one hand. The roads are icy. "You're going to be okay, Sweet Pea, do you hear me?" Daddy's voice shakes. I black out again.

When I come to this time, I'm stretched out on a hospital cot in a small blue room. A fluorescent light blinds me. I sense a pair of hands over my forehead, and as my eyes adjust I see the hands work a needle and black thread. I know the doctor is using the needle on me because I feel the pressure of it break through my skin. My head hurts. My dad stands to my right, his hand protective on my leg.

"Daddy?"

"You're okay, Penelope. You just need some stitches." I know he's been drinking most of the day, but my dad is completely sober at this moment.

• • •

The following summer Dad buys a speedboat so we can water ski. It's clear after a few turns around the lake that my brothers are naturals. Each boy is like a centaur, the skis and towrope a natural extension of his young body.

I'm a different story. I crouch down in the water, knees bent, arms straight, my ski tips pointed to the sky and the rope taut between my skis. When I'm ready, I give Dad the thumbs up to go. The boat takes off but instead of pulling me up and out of the water, my knees wobble, the skis fan out to each side, the undertow yanks me forward and my arms wrap around a solid wall of rushing water that forces me under. After several attempts, I'm ready to give up, but Dad won't allow it.

"You can rest for awhile, but we're going to do this until you get up and ski once around the lake. You can do this."

His persistence reminds me of earlier swimming lessons when I was afraid to jump off the diving board. Instead of letting me give up, my dad made me go back each day to stand on the board and walk a little farther out each time until I was ready to jump. He did not care how long it took me to gather my courage; I was not allowed to quit. Here, again, I know I will have to get up on the skis at least once just to prove it can be done.

It takes me exactly 23 attempts before I finally figure out how to ski. It is almost sundown when I take my victory lap around the lake as the few remaining spectators cheer from the dock. I'm exhausted, sunburned and sore, but I am skiing. Dad turns around from his driver's seat in the boat to give me a thumbs up—his grin as wide as the waves in the boat's wake.

• • •

At Mapleview, I feel loved and accepted by all the other kids. It isn't that way at home in St. Francis. I am an awkward teen and kids tease me about three things: my eyes, my hair and my skin. I can't change any of them, but I try to fight the losing battle anyhow. All I want is to fit in enough at school so I remain invisible.

Some kids call me "Fish Eyes." I don't think my eyes are all that big, but it's not hard to believe that I look wide-eyed. After all, there is the persistent dread I feel in my gut.

Then there's my hair. It's so curly that someone writes in the junior high graduation prophecy that I will someday be the president of Afro Sheen. All the other girls wear their hair long, straight and parted down the middle, so I try my best to fit in. Every morning I go through the same routine: shower, wash my hair, brush my teeth, get dressed. Then I set up the ironing board in the living room. I turn the iron on high and let it heat up for a few minutes while I blow-dry my hair. I get my hair as dry and straight as possible using a flat brush, and then I drop the ironing board to a level where I can comfortably kneel next to it.

I lay sections of my hair on the board with my left hand and hold the iron with my right. I iron my hair one section at a time with the constant smell of burning hair and misty water filling my nose as I lean my head against the metal edge of the board. The white cord sometimes gets caught on the edge and I awkwardly bump my forehead with the hot iron. By the time I'm finished I will have three or four red triangle-shaped burns around my hairline, but at least my hair is straight.

My skin is fragile and pink and I am covered with freckles—especially on my face. When they aren't teasing me about my hair, the boys call me Albino. I constantly complain to my parents that I am allergic to the sun, and it is true. I break out into a rash after only a few minutes outside on a nice day, but my parents have no sympathy about it. One day they plan a boat trip down the Chain of Lakes in Eagle River with two other families. I do not want to go on this trip and beg to stay back at Mapleview. My mom and dad think I use the sun as an excuse to get out of "family time."

"You don't get enough sun," Mom says. "Your skin needs to toughen up and get used to it."

By this time, I have suffered through many types of sunburn. I am intimately familiar with the pain and discomfort and do all I can to avoid it. I come out of my bedroom wearing jeans, a long-sleeve shirt and a hat for cover on the boat trip.

Mom frowns at me as she brushes her long, straight hair. She has a perfect tan. Of course she doesn't understand. "Quit being so dramatic. Go change into shorts right now."

"I can't be in the sun for that long," I argue. "I'll get a bad sunburn."

"You're doing this on purpose, just to spite us and to make us look bad in front of our friends. Go change NOW."

"Do what your mother says," my dad chimes in.

Midday we stop and tie the three boats together for a lunch break. I am miserable as I help my mom unpack the cooler. My skin is raw, red and rashy and seems to be getting worse by the minute as the glare of the hot August sun beats down on the water. At this moment, I hate my mom, my dad and everyone else in sight. I sit in the boat and pout. Everyone ignores me. They are having the time of their lives.

Dancing with Bobby Kayser at the Mapleview Lodge, New Year's Eve 1975.

CHAPTER 4
Mapleview

Mapleview is the first place I discover boys. One winter, Bobby Lee buys me a tiger's-eye friendship ring for Christmas. I spend the next week on the back of his snowmobile during trail rides and sing "Paper Roses" into his ear as the ring cuts into my finger under my mittens.

At 14, my real first crush is Bobby Kayser. We're the same age and our parents are close friends. The Kaysers live in Chicago and we see them often in the city. At Mapleview, I sometimes spend the night at the Kaysers' trailer with Bobby's sister Patty, who is a few years younger. Patty and I sleep on the pull-out sofa bed in the living room, directly behind Bobby's room, which is at the front of the trailer.

The night before Thanksgiving, Patty snores next to me on the sofa bed. I've got the lamp on while I read. The trailer is quiet, but a light shines underneath Bobby's door so I know he's awake. I try to concentrate on my book. As I'm about to give up and turn off the light, Bobby's door opens.

"Hey, you're still awake," Bobby says as he walks past me on his way to the bathroom.

"Uh huh," I murmur. I keep my eyes on my book.

When he returns, Bobby sits in the chair next to the sofa bed.

He wears jeans and a flannel shirt, his feet are bare and he rubs them together. It's cold.

"What are you reading?" Bobby asks.

I hide my mom's *Stiletto* paperback under the blanket. I'm too embarrassed to tell Bobby I'm reading the trashy novel.

"Nothing great," I reply. My face flushes.

"Hey, I don't want to wake Patty," Bob whispers. "Let's go in my room."

I follow Bobby into his room. It's not unusual. When we see each other in Milwaukee or Chicago, the two of us hang out together in our bedrooms and read and listen to music. Bobby puts Elton John's *Don't Shoot Me I'm Only the Piano Player* on the turntable and sits on his bed. I sit on the stuffed chair in the corner, hug my knees to my chest, and sing along to "Daniel," my favorite Elton song. Occasionally we say a few words to each other, but mostly we sing along with the music.

Out of the blue, Bobby asks me if I ever kissed a boy. I lie. "Of course, I've kissed a boy!" My face immediately feels hot.

"I don't believe you." Bobby says as he stands up. "Come here and prove it to me."

My heart races. I'm terrified, but, oh, I want to kiss him so badly. Bobby is cute in that James Taylor way—tall, with shaggy hair, big brown eyes and dimples. He has a crooked smile and a thick Chicago accent that I find irresistible. I get up from the chair and feel frumpy in my flannel pajamas and socks. Bobby pulls me in his arms. At first we just hug. Bobby is taller than me, and I snuggle my face into his chest and breathe in the clean scent of soap and pine. I shiver as Bobby pulls away from me for a moment. He lowers his face to mine and kisses me. I have no clue what I'm doing. I'm intrigued and mortified that Bobby's mouth is open while he kisses me.

Bobby and I kiss for several hours. We stand for a little while, but eventually Bobby pulls me on his lap in the chair. Between kisses Bobby whispers, "You're so pretty. Your kisses are so sweet. I've wanted to do this for a long time." We finally stop kissing as the sun rises. I tiptoe out of Bobby's room and crawl back into bed with Patty as the first rays of light peek through the slats in the blinds.

Later that morning I tell Mary about my night with Bobby. I feel strangely nervous and Mare and I giggle most of the day and wonder out loud to each other how it will be to see Bobby at Thanksgiving dinner that night.

Thanksgivings are big at Mapleview. The families gather for dinner at the lodge, and Izzy Osiecki coordinates the potluck. She prepares turkey, venison and sometimes bear. Our mothers bring side dishes and desserts. Jerry sets a large plank over the pool table and transforms it into a buffet table for the next few hours. The bar is stocked with fresh kegs and plenty of booze, ice and clean glasses.

Little Jerry builds a fire while the rest of us kids pull the couches and chairs around the fireplace. We drop quarters in the jukebox to get the party going as soon as our fathers return from deer hunting. Dead deer carcasses hang from a vertical log suspended between two telephone poles in front of the lodge with the lake in the background. After supper, emboldened by alcohol, a few of the hunters pull out their homemade instruments and play polka tunes. As a group we dance, we laugh, we sing, we hug and we kiss. I feel love and joy.

This particular Thanksgiving is no different, except that Bobby Kayser avoids me. I'm too shy to approach him, so I stick close to Mary. We sit on the sofa in front of the fire with Jerry, Bobby Lee, and Mary's brother Doug most of the night. Little Jerry is telling us stories and we hoot with laughter. Bobby Kayser comes over and sits on the ottoman in front of Jerry.

"Where've you been hiding, Bob?" Jerry asks.

"Ah, nowhere," Bobby answers. "I think I was really tired last night because I can't remember anything that happened after I went home."

Bobby looks at me from the corner of his eye. Jerry, Bobby Lee, and Doug ignore the remark, but Mary and I find each other's eyes. I am heartbroken.

• • •

That Christmas, back at Mapleview, we spend most of the holiday week on snowmobile trail rides with the other families. Each morning, the men gas up the machines while our moms make sure we are dressed warmly in our snowmobile suits, boots, gloves, hats, and scarves.

On these rides, we have anywhere from 16 to 20 snowmobiles together on the trail. One of the men leads and another takes up the rear, checking to see that no one disappears from the trail or breaks down. We snowmobile all over the Northwoods and will stop at local taverns for breaks. That's when our parents have cocktails, and we drink hot chocolate, play pool and feed the jukebox. Mary and I are inseparable. We are the only girls our age, surrounded by our brothers and the other boys.

There is a party at the Lodge on New Year's Eve. My friends and I take our snowmobiles out before midnight and drive out to the middle of the lake to build a campfire. Bobby and I sit on his snowmobile. It's a beautiful night. The snow falls silently and it's completely dark on the lake except for our campfire and the incredible stars. We see the lights of the lodge in the distance, but it feels like we're on another planet. I'm freezing, but don't want to ruin the moment.

Bobby notices me shivering and says, "God, Tam, you're shaking. He reaches for my hands and slips his hands into my oversized mittens to knead my fingers. I don't know what to say, so I let Bobby massage my hands. The spell is broken when Jerry announces it's time to go back to the lodge for the party.

We walk into the lodge and are greeted by a roaring fire. Our parents are dressed in silly party hats and plastic leis hang around their necks while Ray Price croons "For the Good Times" from the jukebox. Mom and Dad are slow dancing on the small carpet between pool table, jukebox and scattered tables. It's a romantic vision; Mom in a paper tiara, Dad holding her close, one hand on the small of her back and the other wrapped around hers, holding it protectively against his chest. He is whispering in her ear and as I walk past I hear him sing to her, "Lay your warm and tender body close to mine . . ." They are in their own little world as teenagers stream past them shedding snowmobile suits and piling hats, scarves and mittens on a nearby chair.

Every bar stool is taken and laughter from the bar begins to drown out Ray Price. Big Jerry reaches for a switch under the bar and turns up the jukebox. There is Ray again. "Hear the whisper of the raindrops, blowing soft against the window and make believe you love me one more time . . . for the good times."

Mom and Dad continue to move together slowly, their bodies melding as one. I sit on the ottoman in front of the fire and watch them as I take off my boots. When I stand up to pull off my snowmobile suit, I catch Dad's eye and he winks and raises his hand slightly in greeting. I return a slight smile and wave, embarrassed to witness this intimate moment between my parents. Yet, I am happy to see them act like a normal couple in love. The song ends and they part for a moment, still mooning at each other and whispering. The din around them grows as the lodge fills with people.

My friends are scattered on couches and chairs, cups of hot chocolate in hand, cutting up with each other. I distance myself from my friends as I watch Mom and Dad. Charlie Rich is on the jukebox now, singing "Behind Closed Doors." Three other couples join my parents on the makeshift dance floor.

While my friends and I are not allowed to drink, most of our parents turn their heads on New Year's Eve, and as long as it doesn't get out of control, they even buy us a drink or two. Dad and Mom return to their seats at the bar after the Charlie Rich song ends. Dad is ordering fresh drinks for them when I walk up. "Elopee, do you want something to drink?"

"I'll take a Coke."

"You can have one mixed drink if you want," Dad says.

I don't hesitate. "Thanks, Dad! I'll have a tequila sunrise." My dad tells Jerry to make me a tequila sunrise light on the tequila. I think it's a cool drink because of the Eagles song.

I take the drink back to the fireplace area and sit on the hearth. Already I feel warmth spread throughout my body. I look around the lodge and the party is in full swing. A couple of the boys are building pyramids of beer bottles on one table. Mary and Bobby Lee are sitting on the sofa talking. Little Jerry is helping his dad behind the bar. I love everybody in this room.

Bobby Kayser walks over to me, a bottle of Pabst in hand. He's on his third beer, but his parents, who are sitting next to mine at the bar, have no idea he's drinking.

"C'mon, Tam. Let's dance." Bobby pulls me to my feet from the hearth. He is wearing a sparkling crinkly paper bolero on his head and has a green lei draped around his neck. I grab a matching hat from the table as Bobby pulls me toward the dance area. Bobby pulls me to him and wraps his arms around my waist. I reach up, put my arms around his neck, and look into his soft brown eyes.

As Bobby and I dance, Dad walks past us to go to the rest room. He pauses for a moment, backs up, and looks at us.

"Christ, you couldn't fit a piece of paper between you two. I want to see a few inches of space here." Dad pulls Bobby's waist away from my body.

Bobby and I roll our eyes at each other and Dad walks away. I pull Bobby back to me.

"Your dad is a serious drag," Bobby says.

"Yeah." I mean it.

I run my hands through the back of Bobby's hair where it falls just below his collar. Around us, other couples are dancing, all of them holding each other close. We're still slow dancing when Dad walks up to us again.

"Christ." He slurs. "You can't even fit a piece of paper between you. Either dance with some space between you or don't dance at all!" Dad pulls my arms away from Bobby's neck.

I give him a dirty look and stomp away to the sofa. Bobby follows.

"He's an asshole," I say as I plop down next to Mary.

"What now?" Mary asks

Bobby answers, mocking my dad. "You can't even fit a piece of paper between you!"

Mary laughs loud and hard. It gets all of us going and soon we laugh so hard tears are rolling down my cheeks. Our laughter attracts more of our friends to the corner. Mary encourages Bobby to mimic my dad and it becomes our joke for the night: "Move over, you can't even fit a piece of paper between you!" We scream and laugh at each other as we pile together on the sofa.

As it gets later, our parents get louder and we get rowdier. We take turns sneaking into the ladies' room with a bottle of MD 20-20 one of the boys smuggled in. Our parents are drunk and we're feeling no pain ourselves. The jukebox continues to play, and Bobby pulls me back to the dance area for a slow song. Bobby is singing in my ear and hugging me tight when Dad stomps over to us.

"God damn it, you're dancing so close you can't fit a piece of paper between you!"

Bobby and I crack up laughing. I look over to my friends. They're laughing uncontrollably. Dad, drunk as he is, realizes we are making fun of him. I see rage shoot from his eyes.

"Get your brothers and get your coat. We're leaving."

"What? No, Dad. I'm sorry. We won't dance anymore."

"I said, get your brothers." He yanks my arm and pulls me away from Bobby. Dad stomps over to the bar and pushes Mom off her stool. From a distance, I see Mom and Dad arguing as I grab Rick. "C'mon. Dad says we're leaving."

My brothers and I dig through the pile of snowmobile suits to find ours. As I pull my boots back on, I hear Mom yell at Dad.

"It's only ten after ten. You're ruining my New Year's Eve!"

"I'm not ruining it. Your bitch of a daughter ruined it by dancing so close to Kayser. You can blame her for this one."

"But it's only ten after ten!" Mom screams.

"They were dancing so close you couldn't fit a piece of paper between them!" My dad screams back.

After we're bundled up, the six of us walk down the dark road to our trailer. The night air is cold on my face and I look up at the sky full of stars. Mom's voice echoes over the water. "Ten after ten!" she still screams. "I can't believe we're going home at ten after ten on New Year's Eve."

Dad grabs my arm. "You're grounded until further notice. Do you understand me? No snowmobiling, no hanging out with your friends, no nothing. You're not leaving the trailer for the rest of the time we're here."

As we walk into the trailer, Mom is still screaming "Ten after ten!" and Dad still counters with "They were dancing so close you couldn't fit a piece of paper between them."

My brothers and I scatter to get ready for bed while Mom and Dad argue. I brace myself for the fight to get physical, but Dad goes to their bedroom and passes out on the bed. I sit up late, reading on the couch, the faint sound of music and the party echo from down the road. I lie down, fold the page of my book and stare at the ceiling wishing I were still at the lodge.

At midnight, I hear the air horns blare and "Auld Lang Syne" echoes. The trailer is quiet. I'm sorry I didn't listen to Dad so we could still be at the party. At the same time, I'm angry that he makes such a big deal about me slow dancing with Bobby Kayser. He knows Bobby. He is the best of friends with Bobby's parents. We're right there in front of them. And it's not like we were making out, for God's sake.

• • •

The next morning Dad is outside with Mr. Kayser working on a snowmobile when Mary and Bobby walk up. I hear Dad, over the roar of the snowmobile, tell them I'm inside. Mary walks through the door and Bobby sheepishly follows behind her.

"Well, your dad let us come in to see you. That's a good sign," Mary says.

"I haven't seen him yet this morning." I flop down on the couch and pull my legs up underneath me. "Last night he told me I was grounded for life. I guess I can't go snowmobiling with you guys."

Mary spots a spiral notebook on the counter. "I have an idea," she says.

A few minutes later, Bobby Kayser and I are sitting next to each other on the sofa with a sheet of notebook paper pressed between our shoulders. Dad walks into the trailer and we stare at the opposite wall with blank faces. Dad puts his hands on his hips and shakes his head. "You God damn smart-ass kids . . . "

He turns to look at Mary. She is doubled over, holding her breath and trying not to laugh. As soon as she meets my dad's eyes, Mary loses it. She dances a little jig and looks like she is going to pee herself from laughing so hard. Dad watches Mary and tries to control his own laughter. He turns back to look at Bobby and me on the couch. We haven't moved. Dad reaches over and yanks the piece of paper from between our shoulders, scrunches it into a ball and throws it at Mary. Then they giggle like kindergarten girls.

Bobby and I sit quietly on the sofa. It takes Dad a few minutes to compose himself, and he is wiping tears of laughter out of his eyes when he finally turns to me. "Okay, Elopee. Take your smart-ass friends and get the hell out of here." He winks at me. I jump up to hug him. "Thanks, Dad." I race to the closet and pull out my snowmobile gear before he changes his mind.

Dad and me before Homecoming 1977. By this time, we rarely have a nice word for each other.

CHAPTER 5

If I Were the Man You Wanted

In 1976, after nearly a year of construction, our family moves into our brand-new ranch-style house. This is our fourth house in ten years. Dad has renovated and sold the three previous properties, the last one being the house he grew up in. For this final move, Dad divided the lot where his childhood house stands, and our new house is built next to the old one, right on top of the spot where Grandpa Joe Ruditys' garden once thrived.

By this time, my dad works full time as a car salesman at Venus Ford and still keeps his mechanic business on the side.

During the move, I find a worn cardboard box stuffed with letters that my parents wrote to each other while my dad was in the Army. I ask my mom if I can read them. She quickly snatches the letters from my arms. "Stay out of these! They're personal." Mom puts them on the top shelf in her closet.

When she and Dad go out the following Saturday night, they leave me in charge of my little brothers. I make sure Rob, Steve and Rick are watching television with plenty of snacks before I pull out the box of letters, sit on Mom and Dad's bed and dig through them. I expect to find mushy, romantic prose in the faded ink and crumpled pages, but instead I stumble upon words that fill me with shock and dread.

"Kathy said I tricked you into marrying me by letting you believe the baby was yours," my mom had written to Dad.

I read the line over and over: "Kathy said I tricked you into marrying me by letting you believe the baby was yours." I can't absorb it. Then I see the date on the letter: January 1961, the month before my birth. I stare at the date and feel like barfing. My mother was pregnant with me. Dad is not my father? I frantically search through the other letters looking for any clues, but the only information I pick up is a first name: Mike. This won't take me far.

I agonize for weeks over whether or not to confront my mother. Meanwhile, the puzzle starts fitting together. People often comment about how I don't look like anyone else in my family. I have dark curly hair and my brothers are blond. My eyes are blue, my brothers' are brown. My skin is so pale that kids at school call me Albino. My brothers are California tan after just days in the sun. My brothers have the steely Ruditys look. I look like neither side.

Reality sets in: Dad might not be my biological father. On one hand, I feel relief. Part of me hates him. The man is a mean drunk and I have watched him beat my mother down emotionally and physically for years. He abuses me, too. Mom might be stuck, but I always know I will get out some day. I am a survivor.

At the same time, I am enormously sad. A bigger part of me loves Dad in spite of his drunkenness and abuse. All I'm left with now is questions: If my dad isn't my dad, where do I belong? Who is this Mike guy? What kind of relationship does my mom have with Mike? Where is he? Why isn't he here? And who am I?

I know the only way to get answers is from my mom. Our relationship is good as long as I don't rock the boat about Dad's behavior. Usually when I confide in her, she's pretty cool. I grab Mom after dinner one night when Dad is working in the garage and the boys are playing outside. We go into my room and sit on the bed.

My bedroom is my refuge. It's painted bright orange like a sunrise. A colorful over-sized Japanese lantern hangs from the light fixture. The faint scent of Love's Baby Soft lingers in the air. Peter Frampton looks down at me from the poster hanging over my bed, and the Beatles stare at me from a picture scotch-taped to my closet door. A life-sized poster of Bruce Springsteen from the *Born to Run* album runs the length of the inside of my bedroom door. My bookcases line one wall and are overflowing with my favorite novels and *Rolling Stone* magazines. I keep 45s and LPs stacked in old milk crates in the corner next to my turntable, and my clothes are strewn about covering the orange and white shag carpeting.

My throat aches and I'm shaky. I can't look at Mom so I concentrate on picking threads from my bed spread.

Mom sits next to me on the bed. "What is it, Tams?" she asks. Her long brown hair floats around her shoulders like soft silk. My mother is petite, just a tad more than five feet tall, and mostly wears her hair in an up-do to add height. Tonight her hair is loose and she looks younger than her 35 years. "Don't pick those threads, you'll pull the whole thing apart." Mom touches my hand.

I stare at hers for a moment. Mom's hands are rough and raw from working in the factory but still she manages to keep her nails clean and manicured. I bite my nails down to the skin. They're sore.

I spit it out. "Mom, is Dad my real dad?"

There's a long pause. It's too long. Mom suddenly jumps to her feet, red creeps from her neck to her cheeks and I know she is pissed.

"Why would you ask that question?"

I come clean. "I know you told me not to, and I'm sorry for snooping, but I read your old letters."

I've never seen my mother this angry.

"You should be grateful," she sputters. "You have a roof over your head, food in your belly. Dad married me and gave us a home.

I don't ever want to hear you talk about this again. Do you hear me? Ever!"

She walks out and slams my door.

In the following months, my dreams are haunted by a father I don't know. I have no idea what to say to my mother, so I avoid her. I avoid the rest of my family as much as possible, too. I wish I could avoid all my questions.

• • •

The news that Bob Ruditys is not my real father remains Mom and Dad's secret. Mom refuses to tell me my biological father's name, and it will be another decade before I learn any new information.

It's easy now to look back and see this as the time Dad and I begin to subconsciously renegotiate our relationship. Part of me feels isolated by the new reality and I withdraw. I am out of sync with my entire family and I want my freedom. At the same time, the control freak in Dad is terrified that he will lose me.

I am my father's daughter, as stubborn and bullheaded as he is, and when we butt heads, neither one will give the other an inch. As the weeks and months slip by, I dream about my biological father. I romanticize what my life would be like if Mom had married him instead. I'm angry and hurt—a newly rebellious teenager with a wild streak. I have no interest in school, I smoke pot and drink with my friends. I dig the bad boys and, as the song goes, I look for love in all the wrong places. The more I believe my dad will disapprove, the more attracted I am to the guy. A pattern develops.

My fights with Dad escalate. He drinks nearly a quart of brandy most every night. Rather than ignore his drinking the way my mom and brothers do, I call him on it. "What do you know? You're too drunk to realize what's going on around here. How can I get decent grades in school when I have to listen to you up all night with the stereo on full blast? No one can get any sleep in this house."

Dad and I find ways to push each other's buttons. Although my brothers are pot smokers and drinkers and hell-raisers, he turns a blind eye because "boys will be boys." I am the one who raises his hackles. I know which words hurt Dad the most, and he knows how to stab me with his own litany of racist remarks, insults about my friends and name calling. "Hold in your stomach, you fat pig," he throws at me as I walk through the living room on my way out the door. I am a gawky teenager with a poochy belly. That one sentence, repeated often, is enough to send me to McDonald's for a large order of fries. If he thinks I'm fat, I'll show him fat.

Throughout the turmoil, part of me longs to rediscover the innocence of our early father-daughter years. And, at times, there is a glimmer of that old bond between us.

Dad teaches me to drive. Some days we come back from a lesson and I run in the front door, slam it hard and yell dramatically to Mom, "I'm never getting in a car with him again!" At the same time, Dad walks in the back door and clenches his teeth together. "She doesn't pay attention and she won't listen to me. At this rate, she's never going to learn to drive."

The day of my road test, Dad and I take Mom's Cadillac to the DMV. He stands in front of me and puts his hands on my shoulders. I lift my eyes to look at him. I'm scared I will fail the test.

"Elopee, you can do this," Dad says. "You know how to drive. You aced the written test. This is the last stop and then you will have your license. If you pass, you can take the car out this weekend and I'll start looking for a car for you."

During the road test, I drive 25 miles per hour through a 15 mph school zone when children are present, I make a right turn from the center lane, and I flub the parallel parking. Still they pass me. Dad lets me drive the car home and keep it most of the weekend.

. . .

Now that I have a driver's license, I need money for car insurance and gas. I fill out job applications at local retail and fast food joints. Dad comes home from work one day and tells me he got me an interview at Dunkin' Donuts.

"What? How'd you do that?" I'm not sure I like the idea of my dad finding me a job. I know him well enough to know that I will "owe him" for this favor.

"I talked to the manager there—he's a friend of a friend. The job is yours if you want it."

I start at Dunkin' Donuts the following Saturday at 8 a.m. I'm scheduled to work until noon. Other than a short stint as a dishwasher, this is my first real job and first time working in public. I'm nervous. My hands shake as I pour coffee into ceramic cups. I blush when customers speak to me. By the end of the first hour, a red, bumpy rash has spread thickly across my arms, neck and face. I don't know if it's from anxiety or an allergic reaction to something in the donuts, but I look and feel terrible.

The manager calls me into the kitchen. "This isn't working out," he says. "I'm going to have to let you go. We'll pay you for the four-hour shift, but you should leave now."

I blink tears of humiliation as I thank him for the opportunity and back away. I grab my street clothes and hide in the ladies' room to change out of my uniform. Then I sneak out the front door and walk next door to McDonald's to use the pay phone.

"Dad, can you pick me up?"

"I thought you were working until noon?"

"I'm finished now. Please come and get me."

I sit in a booth at McDonald's and watch the rain as I wait. I am determined not to cry until I am home in my bedroom. I'm distracted and miss Dad's car when it pulls into the Dunkin' Donuts parking lot next door. By the time I notice it and run out to meet him, Dad is angry that he had to wait for me.

"Where the hell have you been?" he spits. "Why the fuck were you waiting in McDonald's?"

"I'm sorry," I say. "Please, can we go home?"

Dad screams at me as we drive toward home. "Why did you only work for an hour? What is going on? What did you do?"

"I got fired!" I yell back at him.

Dad, silenced by my outburst, pulls off the road into the airport viewing parking lot. He puts the car in park and turns to me.

"Come here," he pulls me over to him and hugs me.

Tears pour down my face and soak his white T-shirt. Dad strokes my hair and kisses my forehead. "I'm sorry, El, I'm sorry."

I pull away from him and use my coat sleeve to wipe my face.

"What happened?" Dad asks, his voice sympathetic.

"I was nervous." I unzip my windbreaker and show him my neck. "Look, I broke out in hives."

"Hives?"

"Yes, hives. Look at me." I look over at Dad. His face is contorted as he tries to hold back his laughter.

I try to hold back my own smile. "It's not funny!"

"Hmmmm . . . hives. . . ." Dad purses his lips together.

"I think I scared the customers."

"Oh no, I'm sure they're used to girls covered with big red rashes serving them coffee and donuts."

Dad and I crack up. I laugh so hard my side aches. I'm doubled over trying to catch my breath when Dad snorts. I howl louder. It takes us several minutes to compose ourselves enough to continue the drive home. As we drive, Dad turns up Charlie Rich on the 8-track player and sings to me: "Hey, did you happen to see the most beautiful girl in the world . . . and if you did, was she crying, cryyyyyiiinnnngggg."

. . .

A few weeks later Dad gets me an interview at Taco Bell. I look at him incredulously for a long minute before I reply. "Are you serious?"

"Of course. What's wrong with Taco Bell?"

"Don't you remember what happened at Dunkin' Donuts? I'm not going through that again."

"El, you can't be afraid of getting another job. The best thing is to get right back on the horse. You said you wanted to get a job and you're going to get one—at Taco Bell or somewhere else."

The interview at Taco Bell goes well and I'm hired to work the 5 p.m. to 8 p.m. shift a couple nights a week. The night shift manager is Dan "DG" Plevak, an older boy from my neighborhood. When I show up at work the first night, DG is surprised to see me. "Is that little Tammy Ruditys? Wow, you're all grown up and beautiful."

I blush, but feel some measure of comfort that I'll work with DG. He shows me the ropes, and encourages me each step of the way. DG allows me to work in the back kitchen the first few nights to give me time to adjust to the environment before I have to face customers. I boil pinto beans and drill them into paste, fry ground beef in oversized steel pans, chop vegetables, wash dishes and observe the counter people taking orders at the registers. Dad breathes a sigh of relief each night when I return from work.

"How was it?" He asks.

"Good. I like it," is my standard answer.

DG eases me into working at the counter and within a couple of weeks I'm comfortable taking orders, talking to customers, preparing food and working the register. I like the work and fit in easily with my co-workers. They're mostly kids my age. This might work out.

Dave Murray, me and my best friend Mary Molter at the Mapleview Lodge 1977.

CHAPTER 6

Breaking Away

One Saturday afternoon that spring I take the Caddy out cruising with my friend Kay. My dad's rule is that I have to bring the car home with the gas gauge at the same level as when I leave. Kay and I stop to pump gas in the car. I put a few bucks of unleaded in the tank, pay the attendant and buy a couple of Cokes for Kay and me. When I come back to the car, Kay is fiddling with the radio and finds the Eagles "Hotel California." I turn it up loud as I start to pull away from the gas tank. I turn sharply to the right, misjudging the cement barrier around the tank, and crunch the passenger side of Mom's Caddy.

"Shit!" I shift into park.

I jump out of the car and run to the other side. Kay tries to open her door, but it won't work. She crawls over my seat and walks around. Kay looks at me.

"What are you going to tell your dad?"

I cross my arms over my chest and try to prevent myself from shaking.

"The truth." What else could I tell him? "I guess this means I'm not going to get my own car. Shit."

I drop Kay off. Before going home, I stop to see our neighbor Scott. He lives around the corner from us. Scott is my age and has recently restored a Super Bee. He knows cars. I bring him outside to look at the damage to the Caddy.

"What do you think?" I ask. I hope Scott will tell me it's not that bad.

"I think your dad is going to kill you," Scott says matter-of-factly. "Want me to go home with you?"

"No, I better face this alone."

I leave Scott's and drive around the corner to our house. I park the car on the street so Dad can't see the damage. As I walk up the driveway dodging several parked Harley Davidson motorcycles, the stereo blares Elvis Presley singing "Burning Love." My dad is in the backyard with his biker friends drinking beer and playing horseshoes. A boy from school once said that my dad would only need a white jumpsuit and he'd be Elvis. I had to agree. Scott leans against the side of our garage where my dad can't see him and gives me a thumbs-up to wish me luck.

"Hi El," Dad grins, his eyes hidden behind the Elvis shades. I sit on the picnic table bench next to Mom and debate my next move. "Elopee, get me a beer, would ya?" Dad asks

The task gives me another minute to figure out what to say. I walk to the garage and grab a Pabst Blue Ribbon from the refrigerator, tap on the top of it with two fingers, and yank off the pull tab. I hand the beer to Dad. He's in a good mood.

"Thanks El." He smiles. "You didn't get my white walls dirty did you?" My father has a thing about white wall tires.

I try to find my voice. "Uh, Dad, I had a little accident with the car." I close my eyes and brace myself for the explosion. I open them again when there is no immediate reaction. Dad stands calmly before me.

"Hmmmm," Dad says. "Let's go take a look."

We walk down the driveway and Dad casually throws his arm

around my shoulders. I try to explain how I crunched the side of the car on the cement barricade.

"Is there any damage at the gas station?" Dad asks.

"No, the cement doesn't have a scratch on it."

Dad laughs. He actually laughs. I feel like I'm in the twilight zone.

We survey the damage. "Yeah, we need a new fender and door," Dad says as he brushes his hand over the massive dent. "I can probably find these parts at a junkyard for a hundred bucks. I can fix it, but you're going to have to pay me back for the parts, okay?"

That's it? Still in the twilight zone, I nod my head yes. I can't believe he is reasonable about this. Just two weeks earlier I had been grounded for washing the wrong work shirt for him. Today I come home after smashing up the car and he's completely calm.

I'm suspicious. "So, I'm not grounded?" I ask.

Dad grabs me and hugs me. "No, El, you're not grounded. But, promise me you'll be more careful and pay attention when you drive, okay?"

Jesus. I'm speechless. "Okay," I agree.

• • •

Days later, Dad throws a cop into our living room wall.

The trouble begins early in the evening when I try to get out the door to go to a concert with my friends. I don't recall my exact infraction, but Dad screams and hollers at me. He's in a drunken rage.

"I said you're fucking grounded and you're not going out!"

"I didn't do anything wrong and I am going to the concert!" I shriek back at him.

Dad erupts into a fury and corners me in the living room. He holds a heavy vase, his arm drawn back like he's holding a football and threatens to smash me over the head. I cower next to the wall and hold my arms above my head for protection while Dad screams obscenities at me and Johnny Cash sings "Ring of Fire" in the background ". . . and it burns, burns, burns, the ring of fire, the ring of fire."

Mom must believe he is going to kill me this time because she calls the police. Our house is a regular domestic disturbance stop for the St. Francis Police Department: usually it is because one of us kids calls when we think Dad is about to kill Mom. Luckily, the police station is less than a block away and Officer Wayne Cameron busts through the front door in a matter of minutes.

"Bob, put the vase down. You're not going to hurt your daughter," Cameron says calmly as he walks over to my dad.

"She's not my daughter," Dad shouts, "She's just some slut who lives here." I flinch as each word rips into my gut like a jagged hunting knife. Pity shines in Officer Cameron's eyes as he calmly places his hand on Dad's shoulder. As Cameron's guard is down, Dad grabs the tall policeman and launches him into the wall. Cameron's head makes a perfect imprint in the plaster. Dad goes to jail for the night.

• • •

After this holy mess, I don't press Dad about getting my own car, but a few weeks before we go to Mapleview for the summer Dad pulls in the driveway with a 1972 Cutlass Supreme Super Sport.

He installs an 8-track player and speakers in the Cutlass and lets me drive it the 250 miles to Mapleview. It is the first summer I experience the freedom to explore Eagle River and the surrounding area in a car. We still have parties at Mapleview, but now my friends and I are free to roam around town with the locals and tourists.

I refer to that summer as The Summer of KISS. My friends Heidi and June are into the KISS *Destroyer* album, and they get me hooked. We cruise the strip in Eagle River in my Cutlass with the 8-track player cranked up as loud as it will go. We know all the words to every song on the album. and sing: "Shout it, shout it, shout it out looouuuudddd . . ." and "Flaming Youth will set the world on fire . . ." and "Beth, I hear you calling, but I can't come home right now . . . " and "You like my seven-inch leather heels and going to all of the shows . . ." and "I'm the king of the nighttime world . . ."

My curly hair is long, big and wild from swimming and humidity, I live in my swimsuit, cut off shorts and Dr. Scholl's sandals. I wear oversized Jackie O. sunglasses and Bonne Belle Strawberry lip smacker. I drive the Cutlass with bare feet. My right foot does all the work, and I prop my left leg up on the dashboard and hang my painted toenails out the window. We are sweet sixteen and we are cool.

Mark Mudler and I have an intense love affair that summer. We had already known each other because his family had been coming to Mapleview for years. When I was 11 and Mark was 10, he chased me into the lake and tried to show his affection like any other boy—by rubbing his poison ivy all over me. The Mudlers don't have a permanent trailer at Mapleview, but they come to the resort to camp several weeks each summer. My relationship with Mark is sometimes romantic and sometimes not, but our friendship is solid and I come to trust Mark completely. He is an old soul, wise beyond his years, and he becomes a true confidant. Although we only see each other a few weeks each summer, we stay connected through letters and phone calls throughout the year.

I drink excessively for the first time during the Summer of KISS. I have had sips of beer and sweet mixed drinks before, but now I scheme with Mary to find any and all alcohol. I think drinking and smoking makes me cool. I take up smoking Merit menthol cigarettes and develop a taste for Boone's Farm Tickle Pink wine.

Bobby Lee shows up at the tree house with a fifth of blackberry brandy and a bottle of Mogan David 20-20. Mary and I sip the blackberry brandy but decide the Mad Dog is more our speed. We drink more than half the bottle, and we're both feeling it when we walk through the campground. The night is black and we shine our small flashlight at a darkened tent where we saw four boys setting up camp earlier that day.

"Boys, boys, boys!" Mary calls as we pass the tent. Mary still looks like she's about twelve years old in her shorts and white bobby socks.

"Quick, turn on a light, there are chicks out there!" The boys fumble around the tent and then stumble out one by one. They are shadows in the dim light of our flashlight.

"C'mon over," one of them calls and Mare and I walk over to the tent.

"How's it goin'?"

"It's all cool."

"Yeah? Great. We're going to build a fire. Want to hang out with us?"

Mary and I sit in lawn chairs next to the fire pit while one of the boys starts the fire.

"What are your names?" I ask. "Where are you from?"

"I'm Randy. We're from Sheboygan. Hey, there's beer in the cooler over there."

Randy brings out a package of Oreo cookies, and Mary polishes them off one by one. We sit in front of the fire with these boys, all strangers to us, and drink beer until the cooler is empty. I stumble home about the same time I hear Dad head down the path as he sings: "Show me the way to go home, I'm tired and I want to go to bed, I had a little drink about an hour ago and it went right to my head."

Tonight, I have something in common with my dad. We're both drunk.

• • •

The fall of my junior year of high school I meet Chris, who is 18 years old and out of school. Chris is what we call "foxy": he's tall with shaggy blond hair, sea-green eyes and a beautiful smile. I fall hard for him. Some days he picks me up at lunch, and I skip school to spend the afternoon with him. We park ourselves on Chris's living room couch, roll a joint, get high and listen to our favorite 70s singer-songwriters: Carole King, Guy Clark, Elton John, John Fogerty, the Eagles, the Byrds, Bread, Billy Joel. A friend of Chris's works at the Esquire Theater downtown, and we spend long nights at the movie theater with bottles of Boone's Farm wine and R-rated movies. As much as I hate my father, I have become just like him. I am drowning myself in music and booze and men, gathering crumbs of love wherever I can find them.

I spend a good part of every day and night with Chris. My dad hates him with a passion. It isn't until years later that I think Dad's scorn for Chris might be because he has an Italian last name, and maybe Chris reminds Dad of my biological father.

My parents question why Chris dates a high school junior like me when he's already out of school.

I scream at him: "You're not my father and you can't tell me what to do!"

Dad yells back at me, "I'm glad you're not my daughter, you're a bitch!"

I know one of Dad's hot buttons is when I date a boy he doesn't like. I taunt him regularly, and promise to move out on my eighteenth birthday with the first guy who asks me.

"I'll do what I want when I'm 18, I don't care if you disown me. No one will ever tell me what to do again!"

I am rarely without a boyfriend, but I am not yet sexually active. My dates involve plenty of passionate necking, but I am prudish about being touched and, other than some feeling-up with Mark Mudler, boys don't get too far with me. Yet, I don't want my dad to know that I am chaste.

One night, after a date with Chris, I come home with a hickey on my neck. Chris is hesitant about giving me a hickey, but I persuade him because I know it will send my dad into a tailspin.

"What the fuck is that on your neck?" Dad screams when he sees it.

"They call it a hickey. Haven't you ever seen one before?" I taunt.

He slaps me hard across the face. "That dago son-of-a-bitch," my dad says.

"I hate you!" I yell as I stomp down the hall to my bedroom.

"You'll pay, you'll pay for being such a bitch to me." I hear his words as I slam my bedroom door.

Chris feels like a pawn in my game with my dad. He breaks up with me. I'm devastated until we get to Mapleview for Thanksgiving and I spot Dave Murray at the lodge. Dave's family has a cottage down the river from Mapleview, and they spend a lot of time at the resort. Dave has long, dishwater-blond hair, and the sexy way he smokes his cigarette is irresistible to me. Dad knows all about the reputation of the Murray boys and forbids me to hang around with Dave, but I leave with him the first chance I get. I imagine Dave is dangerous and sexy, the ultimate bad boy. He communicates more with his eyes than with words, and I like what his eyes say.

As we walk through the woods side by side, instead of slinging his arm across my shoulders the way other boys do, he keeps his hand on the small of my back. When we get to a clearing at the top of the ski hill, Dave stops and leans in to kiss me as naturally as if he's done it hundreds of times before.

Without saying a word, Dave pulls two cigarettes from the pack in his pocket, puts them in his mouth, lights both of them and hands one to me as he exhales. He smirks as he scrutinizes me from the wool cap on my head down to my hiking boots.

"You've grown up nicely," Dave says.

Standing before me is a boy I've known since I was a little kid. As the wind whistles through the pines around us, I shiver and feel both excited and apprehensive about Dave. "Thanks," I answer. "You look pretty good yourself."

"You know your old man is going to have a heart attack if he catches us together."

It's a statement, not a question, but I answer him anyway. I'm defiant. "I don't care. He doesn't own me."

Dave seems amused by me. He smiles. Never taking his eyes from mine, he finishes his cigarette without another word. He stamps both butts out in the snow and pulls me into his arms. As we kiss, Dave pulls the hat from my head and tangles his fingers in my curls. I think I'm in love.

• • •

Later, Dave and I pull up to the lodge on my snowmobile. Bobby Kayser stands on the porch of the lodge. He watches us get off the snowmobile and calls me over.

"What are you doing with him?" Bobby asks me.

"We just went for a ride," I answer.

"I don't think your dad would be too happy to see you with Dave Murray. Isn't he a little rough for a nice girl like you?"

"I am not a nice girl, Bobby." I sneer at him. "Why do you care if I'm with Dave? He's a cool guy. What, are you going to narc on me?"

"Hey, I'm just trying to watch out for your ass. Screw it. You're on your own." Bobby turns his back on me and walks into the lodge.

• • •

When we return to St. Francis, I start going with DG Plevak, my boss at Taco Bell. The Plevak family lives in our neighborhood and, although my parents know DG's younger brother Tony, who is one of my best friends from high school, they don't know DG.

At first Dad freaks out because DG is 20 years old and has a three-year-old son. After a few weeks, Dad takes to DG. I think DG probably reminds Dad of himself as at that age. DG has the well-earned reputation of being a juvenile delinquent, but his heart is good and he is always sweet to me. I feel loved and protected by DG. He goes out of his way to respect my dad, bring me home on time and keep me out of trouble.

On a sexual level, our relationship is innocent even though I try everything I can to change that. DG refuses to take my virginity when it is offered. "You're not that kind of girl," he tells me. He loves to hold and kiss me, but will not touch me otherwise no matter how much I coax him. When it comes to alcohol and drugs, DG is not so protective. He takes me to a bar called the Plankinton Inn nearly every night, and we smoke dope together in his car.

A middle-aged couple, John and Fran, own the Plankinton Inn. Their regular customers are the men who work in the surrounding factories and machine shops. It's a shot-and-a-beer kind of place.

There's a pool table and a jukebox, but the only other entertainment is drinking. The first time DG brings me to The Plank, he tells John and Fran that we're the same age. They don't question DG as he's been a regular for years.

My drinking evolves from Boone's Farm wine to screwdrivers to round after round of tequila shots with my new bar friends. I perfect the rhythm of licking my left hand between my thumb and index finger, salting it, licking the salt, drinking the tequila shot and sucking a slice of lime. Lick, salt, lick, drink, suck. Repeat. I don't know how many shots of tequila I drink each night, but it seems there is always someone buying the next round. The people I meet in this small town tavern are my new best friends.

DG and I break up, but that's all right. A procession of other boys takes his place. I sit at my reserved barstool at The Plank for several years. During high school, I change boyfriends about as often as I go through a carton of cigarettes. The more Dad calls me boy crazy, the more important they become to me. Looking for love, acceptance, revenge—who knows what I wanted? It's a pattern I will repeat for the next decade.

Dad bought me this baby blue 1966 Mustang my senior year of high school, 1979.

CHAPTER 7

Independence Day

I wake up the morning of my eighteenth birthday and for the first time I feel unburdened. Free. Hopeful. It's a new chapter in my life and I'm hungry to get started on it. I walk over to the calendar on the wall. I've crossed off the days for more than a year. Yesterday it was down to the last one. There is a big red circle around today. Friday. I am an adult. I'm 18. No one is going to push me around or tell me what to do again. Ever.

After I shower, I wrap a towel around my body and pad back down the hall to my room. I hear my family in the kitchen, opening and closing the refrigerator, pouring cereal into bowls, spoons clinking. I close my bedroom door behind me and kneel down to look at my growing collection of LPs, organized alphabetically in my Peaches Records and Tapes milk crates. I flip through to the J's and find Billy Joel's *52nd Street*. I pull the disc out of its cover, blow the dust off and place it on the turntable. I set the needle down on the third track, "My Life," and turn up the volume. I've been waiting for this day and now it's here. My Good Friday.

I don't care what you say anymore this is my life
Go ahead with your own life, leave me alone....

As I sing along with Billy Joel I think to myself: *I just have to get through the next four months of school and then I'm completely free.*

I find a white envelope on my pillow. Inside is a letter from my mom. It says:

My thoughts to my daughter on her eighteenth birthday

Dear Beautiful Tammy,

This is a special day for you, the one that you have been waiting for! Now that you are an adult, so many things come back into my mind.

You were in a hurry to start your life and almost caused me to give birth to you right in the labor room. What a beautiful baby you were with all that dark hair and the dark blue eyes that seemed to get lighter and brighter every day.

Your dad was so proud of you, too. When he heard you were born, he managed to get a leave and hitch a ride on an Army plane part way and then a bus the rest of the way. It was about 10:00 at night on February 11, 1961, when he got to the hospital. You probably won't think so, but he asked to see you first and I hadn't seen him for two months.

When you were small you were so beautiful that every place I took you, people would fuss all over you. On our trip to Oklahoma, you were dressed in a very pretty pink angora sweater set that Grandma and Grandpa had picked out for you and as soon as we were on the plane and I unbundled you, I barely saw you until we landed. You were shown off around that plane for three hours.

You should have seen the look on your two Grandmas' faces when they came down to Oklahoma to pick us up. You had grown into such a "butterball" and they fell in love with you all over again. On the long drive home, I very seldom had to hold you at all.

You were always very smart, ahead of most kids your age. The way you could say and recognize the alphabet and repeat stories I read to you was really cute.

Most of all, what I remember about you during that age is your long, long curly hair, curled so tight that it fell into the prettiest ringlets, so shiny and bouncy. During those years, you were always happy and never any trouble for us. I could always take you any place knowing you would behave.

Of course, during every kid's life, they goof, and I remember the first time I caught you doing something wrong. It was when I just started letting you and Robbie walk to the store for me and one day you two came home with extra candy that you stole from Romey's. Well, the three of us walked back for you two to pay for the candy. Seeing I bought the candy, I ate it, and that day I was a very mean mother.

I don't know if you remember when Dad would take the boys and you and I would go shopping. I would take you downtown on the bus, all dressed up and carrying your purse. On those days, you would act like a perfect lady.

When we lived on LeRoy was a nice time of your life. That's where you did most of your growing up. That is where we lived when we first started going to Mapleview. The fun times you have had there and the people you have met you could never replace in a thousand years. Starting way back when you kids used to play the nickel game, think of everything that you did at Mapleview. I think the kids you grew up with there will be your life long friends.

. . . Then we moved into our new house where we have had a lot of bad luck, which is mostly my fault between the snowmobile accident and being injured at work twice. We also lost Brandy, who affected our family more than anybody thinks. But, there have been a lot of good times in our new house, too! You have enjoyed going

out with lots of boys—nice ones too, working, going out with your friends, getting your driver's license, having your phone, and if you look for the good things instead of the bad, I'm sure you could find a lot more.

I've always felt that you and I have been very close and I enjoy when you tell me things and mostly just sitting and talking with my daughter. I hope we will always be able to do that whether you live at home or not.

Now that you are an adult, all I can tell you is to use your better judgment. Think things through before you do them and if they don't seem right to you, take a pass and you won't have anything to regret later. Wrong things always have a way of catching up with you. Always, always treat other people with respect, like you would want them to treat you. Don't lie because once you are caught in a lie, it's hard to get back the respect a person had for you. This is very important during your whole life.

I wish you the happiest birthday you have ever had and hope you make a happy life for yourself. Don't just rush out and try to do everything at once that you haven't been allowed to do, there's a whole life ahead of you.

Don't ever forget that your Dad and I love you very much and always will. I hope we will always be around whenever you need any help.

> *Happy Birthday, Daughter!*
> *Love, Mom*

I celebrate my eighteenth birthday at Plankinton Inn with my classmates and bar friends. John and Fran are mortified to find out I've been sitting and drinking in their bar for years as a minor. Tony Plevak is home from college and shows up for the party. I get so drunk Tony has to help me upstairs where he and I spend the night in one of the empty spaces in the rooming house. We crash on a mattress on the floor.

Tony kisses me and whispers in my ear, "You'll be alright, Tam, I'm here." The room spins and I slip into alcohol-induced nothingness.

The next morning Tony and I wake up late. I'm hung over and my mouth feels like I've been sucking on a wool sock. Tony and I walk down the street to the diner for breakfast. Dad found me a new car a few months before—a very cool baby blue 1966 Mustang (I had the choice between college and the car, and I chose the Mustang). But, I didn't drive it to the bar on my birthday because I had planned to get hammered and the last thing I needed was a DUI.

I still feel like shit when I walk up our driveway at noon.

"Where the hell have you been?" my dad screams. "We were worried about you. Why didn't you call?"

"I'm 18, I don't have to call. You can't tell me what to do anymore."

"As long as you live in my house, you'll live under my rules!"

"Fine, then I won't live in your house! I'll be out of here as soon as I get my stuff."

"Your stuff?" Dad yells. He is incredulous. "I paid for everything in this house. None of it is yours. You don't have a pot to piss in."

Screw this. I walk away and slam the back door on my way out, hell-bent on having my own way. The Mustang is parked behind the garage. I slip into the seat and push in the 8-track tape of Bob Dylan's *Blood on the Tracks* album. "Tangled Up in Blue" crackles through the back speakers, and I sit in the driver's seat and cry until the song finishes. I cue up the track again as I pull out and point the Mustang toward Kay's house. All I want to do is sleep.

I stay at Kay's for the weekend and go to school with her on

Monday morning. My brother Rob catches up with me in the hallway between classes.

"Mom and Dad are worried about you," he says. "They want you to come home after school."

"I have to work tonight. I'll be home later." I rush away from my brother.

After my shift at Taco Bell, I decide to go home, but only because I don't have anywhere else to go. I screw up my courage and try to sneak quietly through the back door. Mom and Dad are watching television in the family room. They look at me as if expecting an explanation.

"I'm sorry," I say. "I should have called. But, I'm 18 now and I thought my life would be my own."

"Tams, people who love you will always worry about you," Mom says. "It doesn't matter how old you are, it's common courtesy to call and tell us if you're not coming home."

I look over at Dad. He is drinking a TAB from the can. He's stone sober.

"I'm on the wagon," he says. "I'm not going to drink anymore." His eyes are pleading.

"I've got homework," I reply. I turn away and walk down the hallway to my room.

• • •

Less than three months after my eighteenth birthday, my dad has a heart attack. He's 37 years old. Ruditys men historically have heart problems, and Dad's excessive drinking and mostly red meat diet have only compounded hereditary issues. Dad is young and has never been concerned about his health.

Dad is still in the hospital the day of my senior prom. I host a pre-prom party at the house and then a group of us, including my new boyfriend, Sid, stop at the hospital to see him before the dance. I walk into Dad's room in my formal—a long pink spaghetti-strapped dress with a crocheted jacket—and carry a bouquet of pink tea roses and baby's breath. Dad's eyes light up when he sees me. I lean over the hospital bed to kiss him. He looks gaunt and pale.

"Penelope, you look beautiful," he says.

"Thanks, Dad."

"Are you having a good time?"

"Yes."

"Good, I want you to have fun. I want you to be safe, but I want you to have fun. Don't drink too much, okay?"

"Okay."

"Now get out of here. I'm tired."

• • •

Dad's heart attack scares all of us, most of all him. Things change for a short time and he does stop drinking. I finish my senior year of high school with a flurry of activities until we finally get to graduation day. As I walk across the stage at graduation to receive my diploma, I spot my parents and grandparents in the audience. They are all smiling, and Dad has the broadest grin of them, the biggest I've ever seen on his face. "That's my daughter," I hear him boast proudly to the people around him. "That's my Penelope—the most beautiful girl in the world."

Shortly after graduation, Sid and I break up when he leaves for Army boot camp. I spend a couple of weeks at Mapleview with Mary and then join the workforce full time as a keypunch clerk in the accounting department at Louis Allis. I continue living at home with my parents. Dad still isn't drinking. Mom, Dad and my brothers spend much of the summer at Mapleview while I stay home to work.

I work during the day for the remainder of the summer and am out dancing with my girlfriends at the Brickhouse Disco each night. For once, I don't have a boyfriend and I love being out with the girls. It's my first sense of real freedom—from parents, from boys, from school. I work every day from 7:00 to 3:30, come home and take a nap and eat dinner. After I shower, I drink a glass of Lambrusco while I dress in velour short shorts, tank top, and Candies pumps. I rat my curly hair into a Donna Summer afro, put on huge hoop earrings, silver rings, and apply blue eye shadow, the blackest black mascara and iridescent lipstick.

In my car on the way to the Brickhouse, I listen to Bob Dylan, Otis Redding, Aretha Franklin, the Staple Singers and George Clinton and Funkadelic on 8-track tapes. We have a group of at least a half dozen girls at the Brickhouse every night drinking tequila shots and dancing to disco until we're soaked with sweat.

Mom and Dad return from Mapleview in time for the boys to start school after Labor Day. Dad has many doctor appointments and is scheduled for open-heart surgery. Sid comes home from the Army on a medical discharge, and we begin to date again. I limit my nights with the girls to weekends and stay home with my parents many weeknights. My job bores me. I dream about being a writer. I look at catalogs for community colleges and think about starting somewhere the next semester.

Dad has coronary artery bypass surgery in October 1979. He has six clogged arteries, and the surgeons take a section of vein from his leg to forge new paths for the blood to flow to his heart. During the surgery, we keep a vigil at the hospital waiting for news. I don't want my dad to die, and I fantasize about our relationship. I picture us as doting daughter and loving father. Maybe this health scare will change him. He'll stay sober and be so grateful to be alive that his anger will disappear forever.

Dad is in the operating room for many hours before the doctor comes out to tell us he's made it through the surgery. When we finally get to see him in the recovery room, Dad is hooked up to an IV with a breathing tube in his throat. His skin looks bloodless and gray, his chest and stomach are distended and his legs puffy. He looks weak and docile, nothing like the blowhard who holds court in the lodge at Mapleview. I hold back the tears as I touch his hand. In spite of everything, I love this man.

When Dad finally comes home from the hospital, he is unbearably surly. Although he's not drinking, he snaps at everyone for the smallest infractions. The only thing that seems to soothe him is his music. I find him alone in the basement many evenings reading liner notes and looking at album covers while he listens to his favorite music. "Did you know the Rolling Stones are fans of Otis Redding?" he asks me one night.

"Really?" I did not know.

"Yeah, they recorded Otis's song 'Pain in My Heart.' Do you know that song?"

I think it's interesting that Dad is talking about a song called "Pain in My Heart" considering what he's just been through with his surgery. He is still pale and weak.

"Yes, Dad, of course I know the song. I've been hearing your Otis Redding records since I was a baby."

"I play my music too loud, don't I?"

I don't know if his question is rhetorical but he keeps talking. "I wonder if Johnny Cash and Otis Redding know each other?"

I realize Dad is talking to himself more than me so I turn to head back upstairs.

"Elopee?"

"Yes, Dad?

"I love you."

I turn back to him and throw him a kiss. "I love you, too, Daddy."

• • •

Shortly after Dad's surgery, Sid and I attend his sister's wedding. We drink heavily and have a great time dancing with all of our friends. I catch the bouquet and he catches the garter. Everyone tells us we're next. I laugh. I am in no way ready to get married. After the wedding reception Sid and I are drunk in his parents' basement. One thing leads to another and we have sex. It doesn't feel especially good and even hurts a little. It's my first time, and I wonder what the big deal is about sex.

On Monday I do the responsible thing and go to Planned Parenthood for birth control. The doctor asks me about the date of my last period and sexual activity. I tell him and he does quick math in his head.

"You might be pregnant already," he says.

"Oh, no," I reply. "I can't be. He pulled out. It was my first time."

The doctor tells me none of that matters as he hands me an oval package of birth control pills. He says to start taking the pills after my next period, if I have one.

Six weeks later my period is MIA. I'm sick. I vomit day and night. I think I have the flu. I feel crappy all day at work. I can't hold any food down. I take a pregnancy test and it's positive. I take another one. Same result. I don't want to tell Sid. I don't want to tell my parents. I want it to go away.

I don't see Sid for days and I ignore the phone when it rings.

He shows up at my house one night.

"I'm sick," I tell him at the door.

"What's wrong?" He asks.

"I'm pregnant."

I motion Sid to follow me to the basement. This is Dad's domain and he's proud of this room. He's built it with a regulation-sized pool table, pine-paneled walls, fully stocked bar, refrigerator with beer tap and my brothers' beer can collection. I take in my dad's room, my eyes wandering everywhere instead of looking at Sid. When I finally turn to look at him, Sid is backlit by the neon of my dad's extensive beer sign collection. The fake waterfall from the Hamms "the land of sky blue waters" sign is the only sound in the room.

Sid breaks the silence. "Are you sure you're pregnant?"

"Yes."

"Have you been to a doctor?"

"No. Maybe I'll have an abortion," I tell him.

"No you won't, that's a sin!" Sid yells. "You're not going to kill my baby."

"Shut up! Do you want my parents to hear us?" I'm sorry I told him, but I place my hand protectively on my stomach. *It's my baby*, I think. *Not his.*

"Please go, I need to go to bed." I plead.

"Let's get married," Sid grabs my hands and pulls me to him. He tries to comfort me but I don't want to be comforted. I'm pissed at myself. Only stupid girls get pregnant.

"I'll think about it," I say. I'm lying. I just want him to go away.

Sid leaves and I go into the bathroom to barf. When I come out of the bathroom my dad calls me into the living room. He and Mom are sitting next to each other on the couch. I know something is up because my dad never sits on the couch. He's always in his recliner. I stand before them—the firing squad. The way I feel I'd just as soon be shot.

"Are you pregnant?" Dad asks.

"Yes." My head immediately buzzes and I feel faint.

Dad leaps up from the couch. "I knew it! I knew it! You fucking slut! How could you do this to us? After all I've done for you, this is the thanks I get?"

"Bob!" My mom yells at him. "Bob, just shut up. Leave her alone."

I remain calm as I walk to my room and throw some clothes in a duffel bag. I walk back through the living room without a word to my parents and out the back door. I'm numb. There are no tears. I drive to Sid's house.

"Can I stay with you?" I ask when he opens the door.

Dancing with my dear grandfather, Ellis Leavitt, at my wedding in January 1980.

CHAPTER 8

Broken-Hearted People

I move in with Sid's family. Mr. and Mrs. B decree that we'll get married and raise our baby. It's God's will, they say. We must look at this as a blessing. Mrs. B lectures me about eating vegetables and walking for exercise. She takes me to her OB/GYN who is as old as Methuselah. I don't care. I don't want to make any decisions for myself.

After a few days of not seeing my parents, I show up at home to get some clothes.

"I'm getting married," I announce.

My dad is calm. "Are you sure this is what you want?"

I shrug. "Yeah."

Dad's shoulders slump and he turns his head away to wipe his eyes. He looks to Mom, but she's not saying a word so he turns back to me. His voice wavers. "Mom and I talked it over. If you want to have the baby and live at home, we'll help you. If you want to consider adoption or abortion, we'll help you with that. It's your decision, you don't have to get married."

"I want to get married," I lie. I know this is hard on them but I don't care. I can't see my way out. The three of us look at each other with silent acceptance. I move to hug them. An empty gesture.

"Well, you're my daughter, and if you're getting married I'll pay for your wedding," Dad says. Let's start making plans."

I spend a lot of time with Mom and Dad over the next few weeks while we plan the wedding. I want to ask them about my biological father, but I'm afraid to bring it up and more afraid that I will lose them if I do. At this point, Mom and Dad seem to be my only allies. I'm afraid and I cling to them. Dad plans my wedding. He books a chapel, puts a down payment on the Sacred Heart of Jesus Church hall, plans the catering and orders enough booze for the entire city. I am not interested in helping and I let him take control. I find a marked-down dress off-the-rack at Sears. It's the first one I try on.

"Are you sure you like this one?" Mom asks. She tries to engage me in the plans for my own wedding, but I am just not taking the bait.

"Yeah, it's fine. Let's take it."

A few times I come close to telling my parents I don't want to get married. I want to be home in my own room. I'm sick every day and can't hold much food down. I take prenatal vitamins but continue to lose weight. On top of being pregnant, I'm a nervous wreck about what my life has become.

Sid and I find a flat in Cudahy a few blocks from my grandparents. I'm glad to be away from his parents, who are driving me crazy with their stories of a wrathful God. *That's not my God*, I think to myself. I like having my own place and start to fantasize about living alone with the baby. I don't want to marry Sid. I'm already beginning to hate the sight of him. His voice grates on my every last nerve. I hate that he doesn't care about books or music or anything that is happening in the world outside of his own family. I always assumed I'd marry an intellectual—maybe a college professor or a writer. I dreamed of travel and adventures and of someday seeing the ocean and maybe even crossing it. None of my dreams seem possible with Sid.

On the big day, Dad and I stand at the back of the trashy Chapel of the Bells, which looks like a remodeled Taco Bell. The flowers, candles and white aisle runner aren't enough to overcome the fastfood dining room vibe of the room. One side is seated with my family and the other with Sid's. It is no secret that I'm pregnant and this is why we're gathered here today. Barbra Streisand sings: "Love, soft as an easy chair, love, fresh as the morning air . . ." and I feel like I'm going to throw up. My nausea is partly from morning sickness but more because I'm about to marry Sid. In three weeks, I will be 19 years old. This is not how my life is supposed to be.

The wedding will start as soon as Barbra finishes her song. Dad and I stand in the vestibule and wait. How am I going to face these people?

"Are you okay?" Dad asks. He touches my hand, which is trembling and tucked into the crook of his arm. I look at him but can't take the sorrow in his eyes so I look away before he can say anything else. "Yes, I'm fine." I think we both know I'm lying.

"El, you don't have to do this. We can walk away right now. The car is right behind us in the parking lot. I can get you out of here. Just say the word."

"I'm going to marry Sid." It is my penance.

The "Wedding March" starts, and Dad and I begin our long walk down the short aisle. Dead. Girl. Walking. I'm numb as I grasp Dad's brown polyester suit sleeve and we head down the aisle—me in my ugly, off-white, Sears outlet store wedding dress and Dad with his forced smile. Sid stands at the altar next to the minister who doesn't know us. When I reach Sid, I smell the booze on his breath. My sober dad hands me off to the drunk who is about to become my husband.

It seems like almost immediately the minister says, "I now pronounce you man and wife," and Sid kisses me. I still feel nothing. I turn to look at Mom and Dad. They know. They know and they let me make this decision on my own. I feel tenderness toward them. God knows they haven't been great parents, but they're doing the best they can.

• • •

Life with Sid is unbearable from the start. He drinks to get drunk every night and often snorts cocaine with his brother-in-law. I feel like crap and am so depressed I can barely get out of bed every morning.

My great-grandmother Gertie is my solace. Each morning after Sid leaves for work I walk three blocks to Grandma's house. My great-grandfather Oliver died the previous year and Grandma is lonely, too. I'm happy to wrap myself in the warmth of her love, although I'm not sure I have enough to give back.

Grandma Gert is nearly 82 years old and seems to have aged considerably since Oliver's death. Her scalp shines under brittle thin curls, and she shuffles slowly around the house, hunched by osteoporosis. Despite her sorrow, Grandma's eyes still sparkle behind thick glasses and she hasn't lost her playfulness. I cling to the solidness of Gram and the satisfying familiarity of her home in the upper flat above my mom's parents.

Our days together settle into a comfortable routine. We eat toast and drink tea for breakfast and then we play cards until lunch. Grandma mixes up Underwood chicken salad spread, and I toast Pepperidge Farm bread for our sandwiches. Then Grandma cuts up fresh fruit into small bowls, and I spoon cottage cheese over it.

Over lunch, we talk about how much we miss Grandpa Oliver

as his silent xylophone watches over us from the alcove next to the living room. I tell Grandma how unhappy I am. She doesn't have answers for me, but she keeps my secrets. After lunch we watch *One Life to Live* and *General Hospital*.

Late each afternoon, we sit in front of the Regina music box. I hand Grandma the aluminum disks of old hymns and folk songs, careful not to cut myself on the sharp metal punched holes. Often I sit on the floor with my head in her lap as Gram sits at her telephone table, and we both weep as the music plays and stirs different emotions for each of us.

Shortly before suppertime, Grandma Gertie fills a wax baggie with M&Ms and shortbread cookies and sends me home to the dingy flat I share with Sid. The candy and cookies are my comfort until I can return to her the next morning.

• • •

My parents have a falling out with Jerry and Izzy Osiecki. There are conflicting stories about what happened, but Mom and Dad are evicted from Mapleview. This news depresses me so much that I wake every morning in tears after dreaming about Mapleview and memories of my happy life there. It seems the last straw in a long line of events that have conspired to ruin my life.

Mom and Dad refuse to talk about it and will only say that the Osieckis are to blame. I feel like I've been cut off from my extended family. Instead of reaching out to my Mapleview friends, I isolate myself, embarrassed that my family has been kicked out of the place we've called home for more than a decade.

After Sid leaves for work each morning, I lie on the lumpy double-sized mattress that barely fits in our tiny bedroom, stare up at the stained ceiling and feel sorry for myself. I usually have Kris

Kristofferson's *Border Lord* album on my turntable, which is wedged between the mattress and the wall. Every few minutes I reach over to put the needle back on "Little Girl Lost":

See the little girl lost: walking through this world alone
She ain't looking for a lover, she's just looking for a home . . .

Our flat is a dump—even $250 per month rent seems too steep for rent. The thin walls are covered in cheap paneling, the cracked yellowed paint rains down from the walls and ceiling, and the carpet is thin as a worn-out dishtowel. Every day I trip on the peeled, jagged edge of puke-green bathroom linoleum that no amount of glue will hold to the floor.

As I prepare the baby's closet-sized bedroom with a cheap crib and changing table, the only furniture we can afford, I think about my room at home in Mom and Dad's pretty three-bedroom ranch. When we built the house I was in eighth grade and Mom and Dad had given me a budget to decorate it. Although they teased me about the multicolored shag carpeting and bright orange paint I picked out, they let me make it my own.

During these early months in my marriage to Sid, I am torn between tenderness and anger when it comes to my parents. Part of me is so homesick that I can't accept that I am living here, in this horrible place, with a boy I hate, when my beautiful room at home is just blocks away. I grieve the loss of my childhood and the broken promise of my future.

Yet, I am so angry—especially about Mapleview. I am convinced that my dad or one of my brothers did something incredibly stupid to get kicked out of Mapleview after my dad's long friendship with Jerry.

• • •

I go into labor before dawn on a Sunday morning in August 1980. It's one of the hottest summers on record in Milwaukee. My pregnant body is scrunched ungracefully on the loveseat in our living room while Sid snores loudly in the bedroom. We had spent most of Saturday at a birthday party for Sid's brother-in-law. I beg Sid not to drink that day as I am already a week past my due date and I want him to be sober.

"You've been saying this for a week and nothing's happened," Sid says. "Today, I'm going to have a good time."

I wonder what I ever saw in Sid. My friends think he's cute and I once thought I loved him. I can no longer see the Sid that used to make me laugh, the boy from high school who held me tenderly and told me he would always take care of me. Maybe my pregnancy and our young marriage dashed Sid's dreams, too. We've known each other for less than two years and I see only ugliness when I look at Sid now, shirtless, in ripped blue jeans and bare feet. He laughs too loud and long at juvenile pull-my-finger jokes. Sid's hair is matted with sweat. His brown eyes are hard and dull as olive pits, his lips drawn thin and mean across craggy teeth, his nose raw and red from snorting cocaine.

I sit on a lawn chair next to my wasted husband and try to make the best of the day. I grow angrier by the hour, though. At 8 p.m., I push Sid into the car, drive home and help him up into bed. Grateful for some quiet time to myself, I lose myself in a book until *Saturday Night Live* comes on TV. After *SNL*, I scrunch the throw pillow under my head and try to get comfortable on the love seat in front of the open window. A fan blows directly on me, but even at midnight the heat is oppressive.

I doze on the love seat and wake up with contractions around 2 a.m. The contractions are sporadic, but I'm scared. I call the doctor and he orders me to the hospital. Then I call my mom. I think about asking her for a ride, but before I gather my courage she says she'll get dressed and meet us there. After all the trouble I've given her over the years about my dad's alcoholism, I'm too embarrassed to tell her that Sid is drunk and passed out in bed.

A storm blows through and a powerful rain beats on the roof. I attempt to wake Sid, but he's still wasted. I manage to get him up and dressed and help him to the car, stopping every few minutes for agonizing contractions. I push him into the backseat of the car and waddle around to climb in the driver's seat. My maternity smock is soaked through and wet hair hangs in my eyes. A flash of lightning startles me as I turn the ignition on the car. "Geez," I say to myself as I place my hand on my heart in an effort to slow its abnormal rhythm. I take a few seconds to compose myself, and then I turn the car in the direction of the hospital. Sid's mother and sisters talked me into to using their family OB/GYN who practices out of St. Mary's hospital 10 miles north of our home. I would have rather used a doctor who practiced in the hospital where I was born a few blocks down the street.

As I drive over the Hoan Bridge into downtown Milwaukee I wish I would have trusted my instincts. I pull over on the side of the bridge when my contractions get to be too much. Lightning flashes and thunder rolls over the choppy Lake Michigan waters below me. Sid snores in the backseat. I finally make it to the emergency entrance of St. Mary's and park the car in the nearest spot to the door.

A security guard spots my oversized body trying to haul Sid out of the backseat in the pouring rain and runs over to help. I tell him I am in labor. When he realizes that Sid is not hurt, only drunk, he grabs my hand and tells me to leave Sid, that he'll come back for him. The guard walks me through the emergency room doors and hollers for someone to come and help. The nurse takes down my information as the guard comes back with Sid, who is slumped over in a wheelchair. When she sees Sid, she runs toward him. "It's okay," I call after her. "That's my husband. He's just drunk." She looks at me sympathetically.

The nurse takes me up to a labor room and the security guard puts Sid to bed on a sofa in the waiting room, where my mom is seated.

I am bent with pain. It feels like an ice auger has been drilled into my stomach. I want my mom. "Can she come in here?" I ask.

"Only spouses are allowed in the labor room," the nurse says.

"Well, my spouse is passed out drunk in the waiting room. Can't you make an exception?"

They do. Mom walks through the door a minute later. She's crying.

"Tams, how are you?"

"Mommy, it really hurts. Please help me." I sob along with her.

"Can I get you anything?" Mom asks.

"How about a gun?" I say, only half joking.

"What's the matter with Sid? Is he sick?" Mom knows. She's been there.

"I don't know. I don't care." I wince as a hard contraction rumbles through my core. "Where's Daddy?"

"You know how squeamish he is," Mom says. "He can't stand to see you like this. He'll be here later."

My daughter is born after more than 20 hours of labor. Immediately after the birth, they take her away and pack me in ice. My temperature has soared to 103 degrees and I can't stop shaking. Every muscle aches and I'm exhausted like I've never felt before. I doze off in the bed of ice.

I awake the next morning in a private room flooded in sunshine. I wonder where I am for a moment before my sore body reminds me. I am hooked to an IV, my mouth is dry, my eyes burn and my body aches with every small move. I haven't seen my daughter yet. I manage to pull myself out of bed and using the IV pole as a crutch, I hobble down the hall toward the nursery. Part way down the hall, I realize I'm not going to make it all the way to the nursery and back. I turn around, go back to my room and ring for a nurse, who brings me the baby.

Sid walks in while I'm holding the baby for the first time. He is dressed nicely, his hair is combed and he looks contrite.

"She's beautiful."

"Uh, huh." I realize he is extending an olive branch, but I don't want to talk to him.

"What are we going to name her?" Sid's eyes plead for forgiveness and it pisses me off. I don't want him near me. Or the baby.

"Jennifer," I say.

"Good." Sid sits on the bed next to me and takes my hand in his. I don't resist, but his touch sickens me.

"I'm sorry about yesterday," he says. "I guess I should have listened to you."

"Yeah," I say.

"So, that's it? Aren't you going to talk to me?" He stands up. I feel his anger rising.

"Sid, I'm tired. I was in labor for 20 hours. Can you please give me a break?"

"Fine. Be a bitch. I'm outta here." He stomps to the door and walks out.

I'm happy to be alone with Jennifer. "What are we going to do, Baby?" I whisper into her soft neck.

An embarrassment of riches: Me with my grandmothers and great-grandmothers at my baby shower in 1980. Left to right: Betsey Buskerud Leavitt, Elizabeth Wasley Ruditys, Myrtle Gertrude Thompson Borland and Jeanne Laverne Borland Leavitt.

CHAPTER 9

A Wide River to Cross

Jennifer has colic. Early evenings are the worst. She cries and cries and the only thing that puts her to sleep is riding in the car. One night in early December, she is sleeping in her car seat as Sid drives around town in our used Chevy, a gift from my dad. I'm in the passenger seat stating my case for getting a job.

"Sid, you barely make enough money for us to survive. If I get a job, it will help with the bills. We'll be able to buy fresh fruit and vegetables instead of living on peanut butter and macaroni and cheese. As Jenny gets older, there are going to be more expenses."

"Who is going to take care of Jenny?" he asks. "We'll find daycare or a babysitter," I answer. "I don't have to work full time, I just want to do something."

"You are doing something," Sid says. He takes the Pabst can from between his legs and raises it to his mouth for a drink. We hit a bump and beer spills over his lips and splashes on his jeans. "Shit," Sid says. He is irritated. "You're a mother and you're my wife. If you want to do something, you can cook more and keep the house clean."

I'm livid. Pissed at myself. How did I allow this? How can I possibly be married to this asshole? What was I thinking?

"I don't know why I married you." Shit. I didn't mean to say that out loud. But, I've come this far and I continue. "Look at you—drinking and driving with our infant daughter in the back seat. What kind of a father are you?"

This sets him off.

"Yeah, you want to see some driving?" He sneers in my direction and presses the gas pedal to the floor. The old Chevy jumps from 35 to 55 to 65 miles per hour on a suburban street with a 25 mph speed limit. Jennifer is in a deep slumber, oblivious to the drama in the front seat, while I'm freaking out.

"Sid! Slow down! The baby!" I stretch my arms out and brace myself on the dashboard. There are no seat belts in this wreck of a car. "Please slow down. I'm sorry. I'm sorry!"

"Scared, huh?" Sid sneers a cruel smile as the speedometer continues to creep up to nearly 90 mph. "Don't have a lot to say now, do you, Big Mouth?"

I've seen this maniacal look many times before on my father's face. I think about how my mother might handle this situation. I will myself to calm down.

"Sid, Jenny is in the backseat."

"Fuck you," he says as he eases his foot from the gas pedal.

We drive home in silence. I'm shaking when I lift Jenny out of her car seat. I hold her close to my chest and wrap the afghan over her face to protect her from the December wind. Sid is yards ahead of me on the sidewalk. He unlocks the front door and walks into the living room. I trail behind him and walk to Jennifer's room. I lay her on her stomach in her crib. She doesn't wake up. I rub her back gently and whisper, "I'll protect you my sweet girl. I promise I'll protect you."

Up to this point, Sid unleashed his temper with verbal abuse. This is the first time I feel physically threatened by him. I think back to all the ways I watched my mom placate my dad over the years. Am I going to have to take a play from her book? I wrap my arms around myself, a futile attempt to hold back the shakes.

That same night, December 8, 1980, Mark David Chapman murders John Lennon. The next day I sit in front of our second-hand television on the lumpy cushion of our garage-sale sofa cradling Jennifer while I watch the news. Tears stream down my cheeks. I feel sad and empty despite the little girl nestled in my arms. I can't believe John Lennon is dead. I picture myself as a teenager in my bedroom at home with a Beatles album on the turntable singing along to "You Can't Do That." How did this happen?

What has happened to my life? I'm 19. I'm married to a man I despise. I'm Mom to this helpless, precious baby who deserves a better mother than me. I have no clue how to take care of a child. I can't even take care of myself.

The doorbell rings and Mom and Dad walk in without waiting for me to answer. I hand Jenny to my mom and fling myself into my dad's arms. "John Lennon is dead!" I try to choke back the tears, but it's futile. My nose runs and tears are hot on my face. Dad wraps his arms around me and rubs my back trying to comfort me.

"El, why so much drama? You didn't know the guy." I cry harder, not sure if I am crying about John Lennon or the mess that is my life.

I'm numb for the rest of the month. I do my best to keep the house clean and cook halfway decent meals for Sid. Jenny and I spend a lot of days at Great-Grandma Gertie's or with Grandpa Ellis and Grandma Jeanne when they're not traveling. A few of my old high school friends are home from college during the holidays and stop over to see the baby. None of them comments on my marriage to Sid, although I know they pity me. I'm jealous when I hear stories about campus life and plans for the future. I once had big plans, too. Now my only dream is to get out of this marriage, but I don't know how.

We spend Christmas Day with my family and I find myself alone with Dad in the kitchen. "What's wrong with you?" he asks me as he mixes himself a drink. "You have been bitchy all day."

"Dad, I don't want to stay married to Sid. I hate him."

"El, you made your bed." Dad teeters and slurs his words. "It was your choice to marry him and now you will stay married." He walks out of the kitchen and I feel hopeless and alone.

My parents adore Jennifer. I can't believe how much Dad dotes on this little baby. He absolutely has to see her every day. He holds her for hours, just gazing down at her and cooing, "I'm your grandpa. Grandpa loves you more than anything." Maybe he thinks it's his second chance with me. His nickname for Jennifer is Jenny-Belly, which is shortened to Bell-Bell and eventually to Bell. He calls me El and his granddaughter Bell.

Sid and I barely speak to each other. Any affection I may have once had for him is long gone. I'm not sure how I'm going to do it, but I know I will leave him.

On a snowy Friday in late January, shortly after our one-year anniversary, things come to a head. I'm still in my flannel pajamas, leaning over the side of Jenny's crib changing her diaper when Sid walks in.

"Did you make me a lunch?"

"Oh, we're out of baloney and cheese. I forgot to tell you last night and didn't have the car yesterday to go to the store."

"Well, what am I supposed to do for lunch?" Sid says, raising his voice. Like I care. "There's peanut butter," I answer dismissively as I finish dressing Jenny.

Sid grabs the headboard of the cheap crib and heaves it across the floor. Jenny bounces on the mattress and begins to cry. "Sid!" I yell. "What are you doing?" I race to the crib and lift the baby to my chest. "It's okay, Baby, you're okay."

"Drive me to work," Sid orders. "Then you can go to the store, buy some lunch meat and bring my lunch to me at noon."

"Okay." By necessity, I understand how to calm Sid's moods. I get Jenny and me dressed, and we leave the house as a family. I drop Sid at work, skip the grocery store and drive straight home. I take Jenny from her car seat. "Your daddy is crazy," I say to her. "We can't stay here."

I pack a suitcase and fill the diaper bag with supplies. Jenny sits in her swing while I study a Wisconsin map. I think about going up north to see my parents, but they are no longer at Mapleview, and I have no interest in seeing their new place or explaining to them why I'm there. My eyes settle on the town of Fennimore, home of my old Mapleview friends, the Mudlers. Mike is in college in White-water, but Mark and Danny still live at home with their parents. A green and white afghan spills over the side of Jenny's car seat next to the map on the table. The afghan is a baby gift sent from Mrs. Mudler. I take it as a sign.

"Fennimore it is," I say to Jenny, as if we came to this decision together.

• • •

We arrive in Fennimore a few hours later. I've never been here, and the Mudlers are certainly not expecting me. I check into the Napp Motel on Highway 18 at the edge of town. I change Jenny's diaper, feed her and prop her between four pillows on the bed. She naps as I pull a phone book from the nightstand drawer. I turn to the M's and find a listing for Richard Mudler. I dial the phone, but-terflies float in my stomach.

Mark answers. "Hi, Mark, guess who?" I push myself to sound cheerful.

"Hi Tam, wow, great to hear your voice."

"Do you know where the Napp Motel is on Highway 18?" I ask him.

"Sure," Mark replies. "Why?"

"I'm there. I mean, I'm here."

"What? What room are you in? Oh man, I'll be right there." Mark hangs up without saying goodbye. Love surges from my heart to my fingertips. I caress the handset a moment before returning it to the cradle. No questions asked. I need a friend and Mark is on his way.

I look out the window a few minutes later and see Mark pull into the parking lot. He jumps out of the car as I open the door. I'm in his arms seconds later. This beautiful boy from my childhood is holding me tight, and I cry tears of happiness for the first time in more than a year. Mark still doesn't ask why I'm here.

"Let me see Jenny," he says as he tiptoes over to the bed. "She's beautiful, Tam."

"Yeah." I agree.

"Okay, let's get you two packed up." I look at Mark and he sees the question in my eyes. "Mom told me to bring you home. You're not staying in a motel while you're here. We'll come back for your car later."

I spend a glorious weekend with the Mudler family. I feel safe and loved. I sleep soundly in the guest room—a deep, restful sleep that I haven't experienced in a long time. They ask no questions and accept me into their home and family unconditionally. On Sunday, I know I must return to Milwaukee. Sid has no idea where I am. Neither do my parents. I have run away from home and if I could stay here with the Mudlers forever, I would. But I know I can't.

Mrs. Mudler asks me to call her Judy. By the end of the weekend she feels like my best girlfriend. The winter sun streams through the picture window that overlooks a peaceful cemetery as the Mudler home wakes up on Sunday morning. Judy and I sit companionably at the table in her sunny kitchen while we drink tea and glance at the newspaper headlines. I tell Judy I'm going to leave for home soon.

"What will you do when you get there?" Judy asks.

"I don't know," I answer honestly. "I can't believe I've gotten myself into this mess."

"You can get yourself out," Judy says. "If you don't love him, if you're not happy, if you feel you and Jenny aren't safe, you should talk to your parents. I'm sure they'll help you."

"They'll just tell me that I made my bed and now I have to lay in it," I say parroting my dad's voice.

Judy is silent for a moment. "You know, it will be hard, but you can do it alone. You're a smart girl. You will find a job and your own apartment. This should be your decision. It's your life and Jenny's life. You need to think of the two of you and what's best for you—what's really best for you. I think you make the decision to go and then stick with it. You'll find the help you need in your family and friends. You're welcome to come and stay with us anytime."

Mark walks in the kitchen in time to hear his mother's last words. He leans down and kisses me on the cheek. "Listen to my mom, she's pretty smart." He winks at Judy. Mark grabs a cup of coffee and sits at the table. He wears jeans and a flannel shirt. His feet are bare and his hair is tousled. He yawns and stretches, his eyes downward looking at the newspaper. My Mark. My beautiful friend. I'm happy to be here. I smile at both of them and feel pure contentment.

A couple of hours later I say my goodbyes and bundle Jenny

into her car seat. Mark carries her to the car and buckles her into the back seat. She coos happily at him and he kisses her soft cheek. "Bye, bye, Jenny," Mark says. He shuts the car door and stands to look at me. "Bye, bye, Jenny's mom," he teases. "I'm sorry you have to go." Mark wraps me in his arms one last time and kisses the top of my head. We embrace silently for several minutes. I don't want him to let go of me.

"Tam, I love you," Mark whispers. "I'm only a phone call away, okay?"

I nod my head, my face muffled against Mark's flannel-covered chest. I break our embrace and look into his eyes. "I love you, too. I can't thank you enough for this weekend. I'll call you when I get home."

• • •

I find my strength in the three-hour drive back to Milwaukee. I say my thoughts out loud to my five-month-old daughter. "Judy's right, you know." I look at my baby from the rearview mirror. "You and I can do this together. I'm almost 20 years old—I'm an adult and I'm your mom. It's up to me to make sure we are both healthy and happy. We'll both suffer if I don't change things. I'm going to leave your daddy. It's the best thing to do."

I sound more sure of myself than I feel, but I know I must leave, I want to leave. The thought of being free from Sid is exciting. I can't wait to be on my own. Maybe I'll even find my biological father and form new family ties. The thought of connecting with my *real* dad makes me shiver with anticipation.

It's dark when we pull up in front of our house in Cudahy. Sid hasn't shoveled the walk and it's slippery with ice and crusty snow.

I walk carefully to the front door and balance Jenny on my hip while I fumble with my keys. I spy Sid through the window. He is lying on the couch watching television. If he knows I'm here, he's ignoring me.

I finally get the door open, walk in and stomp the snow from my feet. Sid looks up briefly and then shifts his eyes back to the TV. It's Super Bowl Sunday and the game is on.

"Hi," I say.

"Hi," Sid answers, his eyes on the television. I've been gone more than two days, with our daughter, with our only car, after dropping him at work Friday morning. He doesn't ask where I've been.

"Sid, we need to talk."

"After the game," he replies, his eyes still focused on the television. Unbelievable. Now I'm just pissed.

"Fuck you. We don't have to talk. I'm leaving you." I storm past him toward Jenny's bedroom to gather supplies. Sid jumps off the couch and follows me.

"You're not leaving me and you're not taking Jenny." He tries to grab my arm. He's drunk and I have the strength of Wonder Woman. I push him away.

"Don't touch me," I scream. "Don't you dare come near me or I'll make sure you go to jail for assault. Or even better, I'll tell my dad how you've been abusing me and he'll kill you. I'm not playing around, Sid. We're finished."

Sid looks like my words have knocked the wind out of him. For a moment, I regret speaking to him that way, but I am determined to leave and am not about to let him get in my way.

"Sid, we can't stay together. We never should have married. We don't love each other."

"I love you," he says. "You're just too rebellious. Ask your dad.

He'll agree with me. Why can't you just be happy with the way things are?"

I shake my head. Too rebellious? I'm resolute.

"I don't love you, Sid. I want a divorce."

Sid backs away like I slapped him. He stumbles back to the living room, grabs for my pink princess phone and knocks it from the table. I watch him fumble to retrieve the phone. He is bent at the waist dialing the phone when he turns to look at me. Tears roll down his face. I'm frozen in the doorway clutching Jenny to my breast. She sleeps through all of it.

"Mom, she's leaving me, she wants a divorce," Sid shouts into the phone.

Oh God, I think. His Catholic parents are going to freak out. I walk away and close Jenny's bedroom door behind us. I lay Jenny in her crib and turn my attention to the chest. I pull open each drawer and empty the contents in a laundry basket. My brain is in overdrive. How am I going to get out of here? Where will I go? Should I take our only car? My dad got us this car so I feel like it's mine. It's too cold to walk and I have the baby. Maybe I should call Dad. No, he's up north. I can go to Grandma's and Grandpa will give me a ride to Mom and Dad's.

The laundry basket is full, but I haven't made any decisions when I hear Sid's parents come in the front door.

Shit, I think.

I leave Jenny's room and close the door behind me. I don't want any of them near my daughter. As I walk into the living room I hear Sid crying to his mom, "Do something, don't let her leave me." He is so upset he begins to hyperventilate. His parents ignore me while they try to calm him.

"Sid, pull yourself together," his mother says. "You need to be strong. You're not going to let another man raise your daughter." Another man?

What the hell is she talking about? What has he told them?

Sid continues to hyperventilate and can't catch his breath. His dad reaches for the princess phone and dials the operator. "I need an ambulance." *Shit*, I think again.

An ambulance—with flashing lights and blaring sirens—pulls up in front of the house five minutes later. I've got Jenny bundled back up and ready to follow the ambulance to the hospital. Sid's parents are hysterical even though the paramedics have gotten Sid's breathing under control and have said repeatedly that he's going to be fine. They will take him in as a precaution, but they believe he's had a panic attack.

I'm exhausted and irritated but follow them to the hospital because I feel guilty. Sid's parents pace the waiting room, still ignoring me. I have no desire to speak to them. I find a pay phone and call the Mudlers in Fennimore. Judy answers on the second ring and I fill her in on everything. Judy calms me down and then instructs me to go to my parents or grandparents for the night.

I hang up the phone and return to the waiting room. Sid stands in front of me with matted hair and his eyes still puffy from crying. His parents are at his sides and each of them holds on to an arm. They form a wall of solidarity as they move away from me to the exit. No one says a word.

Dad with his first granddaughter in 1981. His nickname for her is "Bell."

CHAPTER 10

She Ain't Going Nowhere, She's Just Leaving

My parents find me on the couch curled under an afghan knitted by my great grandma Bessie. Jenny is in her crib in the guest room.

"Elopee, hey El, wake up," Dad says. He shakes my shoulder gently. I sit up, still groggy. "Why are you here? Is everything okay?" Dad is crouched down next to me while Mom stands over him, worry in her eyes.

"I left Sid. I want a divorce." It's a struggle to sit up. I rub my eyes with my fists and with my head bowed I tell Mom and Dad the events of the last few days. I can't look at them. We talk for a few minutes, but I'm tired and can't think straight.

"Get some sleep and we'll talk in the morning," Mom says.

I lie back down and pull the afghan under my chin. Before I drift off, I hear Mom and Dad whisper in the kitchen.

"I'll call a lawyer tomorrow," Dad says. "If she is serious about a divorce, I want to make sure she and Jenny are protected."

"She doesn't have the money for a lawyer," Mom says.

"I'll take care of it," Dad says. "I'll take care of them."

• • •

After my divorce, Dad's friend gets me a job interview at Cutler Hammer, an electronics company that builds components for the military and aircraft manufacturers. I'm hired as a clerk in one of the factory offices. Jenny and I move into a small apartment on Packard Avenue in Cudahy, and a few months later, my friend Barb moves in with us. I love having a roommate. Barb immediately pulls down the heavy drapery in the living room and puts up pretty curtains that let the sunshine in. She buys fresh flowers and stocks the refrigerator with good food. She plays music on the stereo and sings and dances around the apartment when she cleans, which is often. Barb is cheerful about being on her own, and her enthusiasm rubs off on me. We go out on the weekends that Jenny is with her father, and our routine of getting ready to go out is half the fun. Barb pours us each a glass of wine, helps me with my make up, pulls clothes out of both of our closets, pools them together on the bed and puts together some pretty fabulous outfits for two girls with no money.

I go out on a few dates. One night my date, Al, takes me to see the group Alabama at the Wisconsin State Fair. I am completely swept away by the live music and the excitement of the crowd. Al sweetly holds my hand during the show and we share a couple of beers. The intimacy of passing the plastic cup between us gives me a glimpse of what it might be like to have a "normal" relationship with a guy.

Once I am divorced, Dad is especially clingy. Because he is home from work on disability from his heart attack, he stops over to see Jenny and me almost every day. Dad's need to control me, to get me to live the way he sees fit, is suffocating. It feels like high school years all over again. I assert my independence and try to break the bond. I want to be free of his control, free to make my own decisions and mistakes, free to create my own life.

At the same time, I can't deny that my parents are helping me with Jenny. They adore her and she loves her grandparents. The fact that I need their help makes me feel even more trapped.

About a year after I start my job at Cutler Hammer, a new guy starts in my department. His name is Pat and he has recently graduated from University of Wisconsin Whitewater. One day he walks behind me in the parking lot. I'm wearing a baseball jacket with "Tino's Bar & Grill, Fennimore, WI" silk-screened on the back.

Pat catches up to me. "You know Tino's in Fennimore?" he asks.

"Yes, I have good friends who live there."

"I'm from Spring Green," Pat says.

Spring Green is right down the road from Fennimore. It's the home of Frank Lloyd Wright and his beloved house Taliesin. Pat and I talk about the Fennimore-Spring Green region and it doesn't take long for us to realize there is a spark.

Pat lights up a room with his red hair, freckles and easy smile. He is like no other boy I've known before. He's smart, handsome, kind, loving, confident, and hilarious. It is so much fun to be with him. The banter between us is unending and I find myself relaxed and happy when I'm with him. Pat calls me "Mon Petit Chou" (my little cabbage) and writes silly poems for me. Jenny spends one night a week and every other weekend with Sid and that allows me the freedom to build a relationship with Pat. We play together on the company softball team, share candlelight dinners and romantic nights at his apartment, and confide in each other about everything.

My divorce from Sid is still fresh and part of me is terrified of getting involved with anyone, yet I can't help but fall for Pat.

My parents like him, too.

"You'll never find another guy like Pat," my dad says.

Instead of agreeing with him, I take offense. "What do you mean?"

"He's smart, he has a good job and he could get any woman he wants. You should marry him before he changes his mind."

I'm hurt, but I also take Dad's remarks to heart. I suppose because I am such a damaged girl, I have no idea what to do with Pat. Although I adore him, on some instinctual level, I really do not believe I am good enough for him. And I start to wonder what he sees in me. I spend one particularly painful weekend with Pat and his fraternity brothers at the U.W. Whitewater homecoming. Although all of his friends are kind to me, I feel like a white-trash girl at a country club dance. I am so much out of my comfort zone that I spend much of the time sulking and belittling Pat's fraternity brothers for no good reason.

Still, despite my bad behavior, Pat loves me. He says he wants to marry me. He talks about the kind of house he wants to buy me, the kind of life he wants to give me. I'm touched by all of it and I know without a doubt that Pat is the kind of man who would love and cherish me forever.

The problem is, I don't know how to have a healthy relationship with a man. The scared little girl in me wants to marry Pat and let him take care of me. But a small voice inside tells me I'm not ready to get married again. I just got out of a horrible marriage. I harden my heart. I know I'm not good enough for Pat. I'll drag him down. I don't know what he sees in me and I don't believe I deserve him. I do what I can to create distance between us.

Pat puts up with my distance and pettiness for many months, but he's too smart to let me knock him around much more. Our last date is on a bright summer day. We're invited to a barbecue. Pat picks me up outside my apartment, and I hop in the passenger seat and lean over to kiss him. Pat lets me kiss him, but now he's distant. For once, he doesn't smile when he sees me. By this point, I have pushed Pat to the limit with my inconsiderate behavior. His bare arm—strong, tan and freckled—reaches over my leg to adjust the cassette player. As we drive away, he cranks up a song by the band Asia, "Only Time Will Tell." The lyrics are telling:

You're leaving now
It's in your eyes
There's no disguising it

I know Pat is sending me a message. My chest aches and I sneak glances at him as he drives. His sunglasses don't hide the sorrow in his eyes and his mouth is set in a thin line. I know he is upset and hurt. I pick a fight with him. By the end of the day, we are over.

• • •

Dad's mother dies in January 1983. I barely know Elizabeth Ruditys. She is a hard woman and seems nervous when kids are around. Although Liz is kind to me, she doesn't possess natural warmth like Mom's mother, Grandma Jeanne. I stayed with Liz a time or two during high school when my parents were at Mapleview alone. She'd sit at the kitchen table chain smoking and sipping beer from a small glass. The ashtray was filled with cigarette butts streaked with red lipstick. Grandma Liz blew perfect smoke rings above my head. Instead of keeping her beer bottle in front of her at the table, she'd walk to the refrigerator each time her glass was empty, pull out the open bottle, pour beer her glass and return the bottle to the refrigerator.

I think I was a little bit scared of Liz because of the stories I heard from Mom and Dad. On the New Year's Eve only days after they married, Mom and Dad stayed with Grandma and Grandpa Ruditys while Dad was on leave from the Army. Mom got her first taste of what it meant to be part of the Ruditys family in the early morning hours of New Year's Day when her new in-laws returned from the tavern after closing time. A drunken Liz stumbled up to the bedroom where Mom and Dad slept. She flung open the door, screamed obscenities and yelled at Dad to get out of her house. With no regard to the fact that Mom was seven months pregnant, Elizabeth Ruditys tossed her youngest son and his new wife out into the cold and snow.

The evening of Liz's funeral, I watch television in my parents' basement while Jenny naps in the guest room upstairs. The television sound is turned low and the only light is the soft glow from the screen. I hear Dad as he walks down the stairs, but he doesn't know I'm here.

"Hi Dad," I say quietly.

"Elopee!" Dad jumps. "You scared the hell out of me."

"Sorry."

He walks to the bar and reaches for the opened bottle of brandy. After filling his glass, Dad walks toward me, shaking his glass gently to mix the brandy and ice. He sits down next to me on the couch. There is an uncomfortable silence. Dad stares at his glass, I stare at the television.

"I'm sorry about Grandma." I'm not sure if this is the right thing to say. Dad reaches forward and sets his glass on the coffee table. He puts his head in his hands and sighs deeply. Soon his torso shakes and I know he is trying to hold back his tears.

I'm not sure what to do in this intimate moment. My heart aches for him. I put my hand on his back. A moment later, Dad weeps in my arms and I comfort him like I would a child.

"El, you just don't know how it feels to not have parents. They're both gone forever."

We sit there for several minutes, and Dad cries while I pat his back trying to comfort him.

"I'm sorry, I'm sorry." I can't find any other words.

Dad breaks away from me, leans forward to grab his cocktail and drains it in one long drink. Silently, he gets up from the couch, refills his drink and walks upstairs.

• • •

The same week Dad's mother dies, I am laid off from Cutler Hammer. I'm still grieving my break-up with Pat, and now I am unemployed and won't see him at work every day. Mom and Dad tell me I can move back home until I find a new job. I do. A few weeks later, Jenny is diagnosed with a urinary tract birth defect and has to have surgery immediately.

Sid and I both stay in the hospital with Jenny for seven days, and I consider getting back together with him just so I don't have to be alone. Instead, I take a page from my dad's book and start drinking nearly every night, and I fall back into my old pattern of dating countless unsuitable men who drink too much and aren't nice to me. My parents keep Jenny while I'm out nearly every night. On my twenty-second birthday, I return to my parent's house after a long night of partying. Dad and I are both drunk and he blows up at me. We argue and scream obscenities at each other under the porch light. Dad storms to the garage, comes back with a heavy metal chain and throws it into my windshield. Glass shatters on the hood of the car and tumbles to the driveway like a hailstorm.

I realize I can't continue living with my folks. I sign up at a temp agency and work a string of clerking jobs at manufacturing companies. Jenny and I move out to a small lower flat in Cudahy. My brother Rick is a senior in high school and helps me out by babysitting on weekends and during the summer after he graduates. My relationship with Mom and Dad is strained, and I see little of them.

They do take Jenny often, but I'm too wrapped up in my own self-ishness and I never thank them.

• • •

I meet my next boyfriend, Bryan, one night out at the bar. His red hair reminds me of Pat. There is something calming about Bryan that I like. Bryan is shy and grounded and I am a flighty party girl always looking for fun—he calls me his "Wild Child." Somehow we make it work and after more than a year of dating we move in together.

My family loves Bryan and his easygoing nature. Although Bryan has a soothing affect on me, I have a problem with his tight relationship with my parents. My own is as thin and tenuous as a spider's web. It is Jenny's and Bryan's bond with my family that keeps me connected at all. Things are always tense between Dad and me and adding to my distress is that Bryan takes Dad's side over mine in many arguments. Bryan is like my mother in that he wants me to let my dad's ravings "go in one ear and out the other."

Much of the time, I feel like I may drown under the weight of their judgments—and now Bryan and his expectations of me.

My dad's nickname for Bryan is DB, short for Dick Breath. It is inconceivable to me that Bryan laughs this off. Eventually, my brother Rick gets in the act and the three of them call each other vulgar nicknames.

Yet, many aspects of my life with Bryan comfort me. He and Jenny adore each other, I feel a sense of security and stability, and I don't think Bryan is too good for me in the way I believed about Pat. I am not sure I love Bryan and I still miss Pat, but Pat has moved on. Deep down inside, I feel like I am giving up and giving in, but I don't have the will to find my own way.

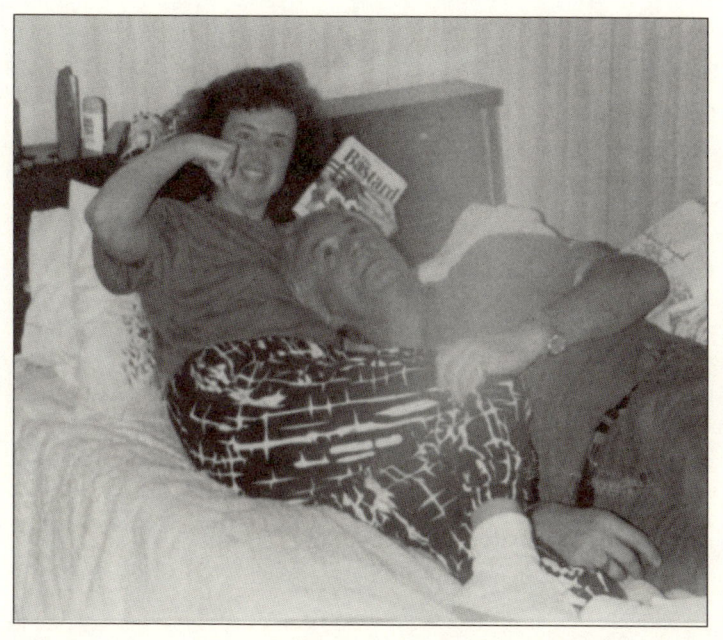

In a light-hearted moment with Dad in the early 1980s.

CHAPTER 11

Sister Lost Soul

The Saturday before Halloween when she is five years old, Jenny spends the night with Bryan's twin nieces and their family. The next morning, after taking my grandmother to church, I drive to Oak Creek to pick her up. The twins' mom, Amy, meets me in the driveway.

"I have to talk with you before you see Jenny."

Her solemn expression makes me panic. "What happened? Is Jenny okay?"

Amy places her hand on my arm. "Last night Jenny told the girls that her dad touches her . . . in her private parts."

This takes a minute to sink in. "What? That can't be. Wait, what exactly did she say?"

Amy tells me she didn't hear the conversation. The twins had come to her with the information and Amy did not question Jenny. Amy seems to speak in slow motion and her words don't reach me. Thoughts dash around inside my head like Wile E. Coyote chasing the Road Runner.

Oh my God. Oh my God. Maybe it's a mistake. Maybe he just touched her when he was bathing her. But what if he did hurt my baby? Oh my God. No. No. Nooooo!

"I have to go." I push Amy away. "I have to find out what happened."

I pack Jenny into the car and we drive away.

I will myself to remain calm and keep my voice even. "Honey, the twins said you told them Daddy touched your private parts. Can you tell Mommy about it?"

Jenny begins to sob. "No, Mommy, no! Daddy said you'd put me in an orphanage if I tell!"

I pull the car over to the side of the road, unbuckle Jenny and pull her into my lap. I hug my daughter hard and hold her head to my breast as she cries. Her little body quivers between my chest and the steering wheel, and I whisper words I hope will comfort both of us.

"Jenny, you are my baby and you will always be with me. I'll never leave you, no matter what happens. You are my family and we'll be together forever."

We cry together, my little girl and me, parked in the gravel on the side of the road in Oak Creek, along the same route where my own parents took me for Sunday drives in the country. I think about my dad and what he will do to Sid when he finds out about this. We sit on the side of the road tangled in each other's arms for a long time. Jenny cries herself to sleep. I ease away from the steering wheel and move her to the backseat. I kiss her forehead as I lay her down and pull the seatbelt around her thin hips. I gaze at Jenny's milky skin, feather-light blond hair, skinny arms and legs. What the hell has he done to her? She is only five years old.

• • •

I'm not sure about my next move. I pace around the kitchen while I consider my options. Sid now has another daughter from a relationship after ours. He's living with his current girlfriend and they are planning to marry soon—and have children. He has already hurt my daughter—who would be next?

Jenny sleeps soundly upstairs. It's Sunday afternoon and my parents are likely on the drive home from up north. Bryan is bow hunting and will be home later tonight. I can't wait. I have to do something now. I call the Cudahy Police Department and tell them I believe her father has molested my daughter.

Within 30 minutes, a juvenile officer rings my doorbell. He carries two rag dolls—one male and one female.

"These are anatomically correct dolls," Officer Terry explains as we sit opposite each other in the living room. "I'd like to observe your daughter with them. First, tell me what she told you."

I repeat what I heard from Amy and from Jenny. It's not much to go on. I admit I am afraid to ask her any more about it. Before we can continue the conversation, I hear Jenny on the stairs.

"Jenny," I call to her, "I'm in the living room."

Jenny walks in clutching her Rainbow Brite doll and trailing a pink blanket behind her. She looks at Terry shyly as she crawls into my lap.

"Jenny, this is my friend Officer Terry. He's a nice man. Look, he brought some dolls for you to play with."

Terry smiles and holds the dolls out to her. Jenny leaves Rainbow Brite and the blanket in my lap, takes the dolls from Terry and sits on the floor between us to play with them. Terry and I watch her. Terry begins a conversation about the Green Bay Packers' season. We talk football and never move our eyes from Jenny. Within a few minutes, Jenny whispers, "this is the daddy and this is the little girl" as she pantomimes sexual moves between the dolls.

I stare deliberately at Terry and stand up. I excuse myself and exit the room slowly. I don't want to scare Jenny. Alone in the bathroom, I brace myself on the sink and look at myself in the mirror. I think I've failed as a mother. I didn't protect my baby girl. She has been violated in ways I can't even begin to imagine. What will become of us? I sink to my knees and vomit into the toilet.

Terry leaves after taking Jennifer's "statement." He's on his way to arrest Sid. I leave a message on my parents' answering machine. "Daddy, I need you. Please come over here as soon as you get this message. I don't care what time it is . . . this is . . . serious."

I'm numb and on autopilot for the next several hours. I play with Jenny. Feed her dinner. Bathe her. Tuck her into bed. At 9:30 I hear a car peel into the driveway. Dad is frantic when he bursts through the door.

"What is it? What's wrong?"

I throw myself into his arms and sob. Now that he's here, I can't compose myself enough to tell him. I just want my daddy to hold me and make it better. Dad grabs my shoulders and pushes me back so he can look at my face. "El, tell me right now what is going on." I look into his eyes and see his fear.

I recount the day to him and don't leave one detail to the imagination. I tell Dad exactly what Jenny did with the dolls—a vivid picture of what Sid did to his granddaughter. Now I hold on to his arms as he tries to break free. "I'll kill him," my dad seethes. "I'm going over there right now and I swear I am going to kill him."

I have no doubt my dad will kill Sid. I want my dad to kill him. But a sliver of logic remains inside me and I know it is not an option. "Dad, I need you. I need you. If you're arrested for murdering Sid, you won't be any help to me or to Jennifer." I howl like a wounded animal. "Please. Please be here for me. I know he deserves to die, but I can't handle this without you."

Bryan walks in from his hunting trip. He's dressed in camouflage overalls and holds his bow awkwardly in front of him. "What's going on?" Bryan asks as he tugs a wool hat from his head. His red hair sticks straight up from the static. I know Bryan can sense the tension in the room but I'm not sure how to tell him.

"Sid molested Jenny," my dad says matter-of-factly. I've still got a death grip on his arm. Bryan's face is expressionless. He runs up the stairs. I think he's going to check on Jenny but he returns seconds later loading bullets into his revolver. My dad breaks away from me.

"Let's go," Bryan says to my dad. They walk toward the door together, determined.

"Wait!" I scream loud and it hurts my throat. "You're going to make it worse. How am I going to tell Jenny that her grandpa and Bryan are in jail for killing her father? She will blame herself. She'll never recover. It will ruin her life. Jenny needs both of you!"

This outburst takes everything out of me. I collapse back on the couch and put my head in my hands. "Please help me. Please don't leave me." I babble on and on until both men are at my side and the three of us cry together.

• • •

The state of Wisconsin charges Sid with first-degree sexual assault on November 26, 1985. He appears in court on December 19, waives the preliminary hearing and is bound over for trial. Dad escorts me to every meeting with the assistant D.A. and every court appearance. I take a leave of absence from work and my doctor puts me on Valium.

I'm afraid to leave Jenny alone even for a few minutes. I walk her into her classroom each morning and pick her up each afternoon. We spend a lot of time with my dad. Mom works full time, but Dad is home on disability for his heart problems. Somehow we manage to make it through the holidays. We don't talk about what happened but throw ourselves into doting on Jenny.

Sid is arraigned on January 13 and enters a not guilty plea. The case is continued, and Sid faces a jury trial scheduled for March. Assistant District Attorney Gale Shelton explains that a jury trial means Jennifer will have to testify. I'm numb from the Valium.

Dad is livid. "Testify? You're going to put a five-year-old little girl on the witness stand to tell a court room full of strangers what happened to her? Are you out of your mind?" Gale is patient with my father. "I don't like it anymore than you do, but it's the only way we'll get a conviction."

We stand in Gale's office silently. I'm sure we're all thinking the same thing. Sid works as a janitor at a Catholic Church and school in St. Francis. We can't take the chance that he'll harm another child. A status hearing is scheduled for February 24.

Sometime during the month, Sid changes his plea to guilty. I believe he is scared of a jury hearing Jenny's testimony, but we are all relieved that it won't come to that. He is convicted of first-degree sexual assault against a minor and sentenced to nine months in county jail with work privileges plus four years probation and drug, alcohol and psychological counseling.

By the time the ordeal is over, I am drained and floundering. I can find no joy. Each night I sit alone to cry and listen to sad songs over and over again. Bryan and I cancel our wedding, which was scheduled for August. I have no desire to plan a wedding or commit myself to a new marriage. Bryan and I stay together, but I am sick and broken—emotionally unavailable to him and everyone else.

• • •

During this time, my brother Rick checks himself into DePaul Rehabilitation Hospital. He's in his early 20s, but his drinking is already out of control. After he was recently smashed in the face with a tire iron during a fight, his girlfriend Kim gives him an ultimatum. Rick chooses rehab over losing her. My brothers Rob and Steve are already lost to drug and alcohol addictions, and the two of them are constantly in and out of jail. Yet, my parents are so much in denial that they can't see Rick has completely self-destructed. "Rick is not an alcoholic," Dad says. "He may have a drinking problem, but he's too young to be an alcoholic."

Kim and I attend family therapy sessions with Rick. No one else from my family shows up. During the therapy, Rick and I learn about our roles in our alcoholic family games. It's clear that I am, and always have been, the provoker. I still play the part well and never let Dad off the hook or cut him any slack when it comes to his drinking. Mom is a typical enabler. My brothers take up the parts of hero, clown and scapegoat. We each play our roles like a finely crafted Broadway theater production.

I'm physically ill from the therapy sessions with Rick. I ache for him and wish I could heal his pain, but I'm such a mess myself that I barely have anything left for my baby brother. I come home from each session and plant myself on the floor by the toilet. In between retching, I cry. I withdraw from Bryan and Jenny so I don't come unglued in front of them. At the same time, I avoid Mom and Dad and isolate myself from my grandparents and friends. I feel like a sheet flapping on a backyard clothesline—windblown and going nowhere.

After a few months, I join a gym to get away from everyone, but there I run into my old boyfriend Pat with his new wife. Each time I see Pat, my heart feels like it is being slowly and steadily squeezed between the metal plates of the vise bolted to Dad's workbench.

I take up jogging and running becomes my salvation. My body feels strong and my mind stronger when I run. I'm empowered. There is no drama in the steady beat of my heart, the rhythm of my feet on the pavement, the wind in my hair and the miles and miles of Lake Michigan stretched out next to me. I start running three miles a day, then five. Soon I run five miles a day during the week and seven to ten miles on Saturday and Sunday. I'm addicted to the high. I work on increasing my stamina and performance. I stop drinking. I eat healthier. I don't care about anything else. It's just the road and me.

On my twenty-sixth birthday I meet a guy at the gym and we start a passionate affair. I still live with Bryan and Jack is married, but Jack becomes my sole reason to drag myself out of bed in the morning. I'm up at 5 a.m. and at the gym when it opens at 5:30. Jack and I spend our mornings together until I have to be at work at 9 a.m. Sometimes we stay at the gym, and sometimes we just skip it and go to his apartment. After work, I go home to Bryan and Jennifer, but I flee to the bedroom after I put Jenny down at 8 p.m. My relationship with Bryan is almost nonexistent.

I can't see that I am self-destructing. I only want something, or someone, to breathe new life into me.

• • •

I need a moment's peace, but it is not to be. Mom calls late on a Sunday night, after Jenny is in bed, when Bryan and I are settled on the couch watching television.

Bryan hangs up the phone and looks at me. "That was your mom. She's at the St. Francis Police Department. Your dad beat her up. I told her I'd come and get her."

"God damn him!" I scream. I remember an incident from my childhood that ended with Dad throwing Mom down the basement stairs. "I can't believe he's still doing this shit and I can't believe she's still taking it!"

Bryan pulls me into his arms. I shake with heavy sobs and tears roll down my cheeks. I ask Bryan to stay with Jenny while I go pick up my mother.

Bryan argues with me for a few minutes, but is intimately familiar with my stubborn streak. He knows I won't change my mind. He follows me into the bedroom as I'm pulling the top of my flannel pajamas over my head.

"Are you sure? I can just go and bring her back here?" Bryan pleads.

I don't reply as I pull a pair of jeans and a shirt from my dresser. My entire body trembles as I dress and I can't seem to catch my breath. I sit on the edge of the bed to pull my sneakers on. My head falls to my knees involuntarily and I allow the tears to flow, just for a few minutes, just long enough to loosen the lump beneath my breastbone.

Bryan kneels down beside me and takes my hand. I take a few deep breaths, wipe my eyes and Bryan helps me to my feet. My mom needs me. I have to pull myself together. Bryan walks me down the stairs and out to our parking spots in the back of the house. My battered green Ford Pinto sits next to his gleaming new maroon Chevy Monte Carlo. "Here, take my car," Bryan says handing me his keys. "It's more comfortable." I hug him, take the keys gratefully and climb in the driver's seat. Bryan lifts his hand to wave as I pull out to the alley.

A few minutes later I park in the lot at the police precinct. I feel stronger than I did at home and walk purposefully in the door. Mom sits on a bench in the wide hallway. The fluorescent lighting is harsh on her face. Her eyes are red and raw, tufts of hair stick straight up and out the side of her head. Her mouth is set in a thin line. She looks up and realizes I'm watching her. Perhaps she sees the pity in my eyes. She reaches up to smooth her hair and stands up slowly. She doesn't meet my gaze.

"I thought Bryan was coming."

Bryan was a safer choice for her. He would not pepper my mother with questions, he would comfort her and drive her wherever she wanted to go. He wouldn't look at her the way I am: questioning, accusing, and judging.

"Mom, I wanted to come." I say. "C'mon. Let me take you to my place for the night."

I gently put my hand on her elbow and guide her toward the door. Mom winces with each step. She is bruised and battered from head to toe. As I stand close to her, I notice the swelling of her cheek and the bluish spots on her neck and chin.

"Mom, what did he do to you?"

"He was really drunk." The typical excuse slips easily from her mouth. "I talked back and he pushed me on the floor and kicked me."

I envision my five-foot-tall mother writhing in a corner as a 200-pound man pummels her ribs, stomach, back and face. It takes an eternity to get Mom in the car. After closing the door after her, I walk around to the driver's side, breathing deeply and trying to control my anger. I get in the car and start the ignition. We don't speak. I put the car in reverse, back out of the parking lot and head in the opposite direction from my house.

"Where are we going?" Mom asks.

"I'm taking you to the emergency room to get checked out," I reply. "You might have broken ribs."

Mom turns away from me and looks out the window without speaking. Thirty minutes later a doctor pulls a white curtain around Mom and me. Mom sits on the hospital cot wearing a thin gown. Her legs stick out from under the gown, speckled with purple welts. The doctor helps Mom lie back on the bed and touches her around her collarbone before running his hands carefully down her ribs and abdomen. He picks up each arm and gently feels the flesh from shoulders to fingers. As he works, he glances my way.

"How did this happen?"

Mom looks at me, daggers in her eyes, imploring me not to tell. She is a proud woman.

"Her husband beat her," I say defiantly, not moving my eyes from Mom's.

She's angry and looks away from me.

"We should notify the police," the doctor says.

"They know," I say. "I just picked her up from St. Francis PD."

The doctor leaves it alone and Mom won't look at me. I am angry. Blood throbs in my ears. I want to hit Dad and throw him down in a corner and kick him. Beat him the way he beat her. Maybe I'm not so different from him after all.

"There's nothing broken," the doctor finally says. "But, you are bruised pretty badly. You should rest for a few days and come back if the pain doesn't ease."

Mom gets dressed and we make our way to the parking lot. The foghorns from Lake Michigan blow through the stillness of the night. The familiar sound soothes me and my anger dissipates into the brisk air. I breathe deeply. We get in the car and I roll down my window. We take the long way home, driving north on Lake Drive, listening to the foghorns and the waves crashing against the rocks.

Bryan hears us pull up and runs down the stairs to help Mom out of the car. He already has the sofa bed made up for her. Mom says goodnight, climbs into bed fully clothed and turns her back to us. Once we are alone in our room I explode.

"That son of a bitch. Someone needs to kick him black and blue."

Bryan pulls me into his arms. "I'm sorry," he says. "Your mom is safe now. She's going to be okay."

"If she goes back to him, I'll never forgive her."

Of course, I know she will.

Mom and Dad model vintage swim wear at Mapleview around 1975.

CHAPTER 12
The Hard Way

I lay awake and stare at the ceiling. Every now and then I get out of bed and open the door to listen to Mom's breathing from the living room. She sleeps fitfully and at one point I hear her crying.

The next morning, Bryan takes Jenny to school on his way to work. I call in sick and stay in my bedroom reading while Mom sleeps. The phone rings around 10 a.m. and I know instinctively it's Dad. I pick up the phone in the bedroom.

"Hello?" The hard edge in my tone is purposeful.

"Put your mother on the phone," Dad says.

"Fuck you!" I scream and slam the phone in its cradle.

The phone rings again. I should ignore it but instead I pick up the receiver and yell.

"Don't ever call here again, you bastard. Leave my mother alone."

"Don't you ever fucking hang up on me again!" he screams. "I'm so lucky you aren't my daughter. You're just a fucking bitch."

I slam the phone down once again and try to calm down. When Mom stirs, I get up and walk on wobbly knees into the living room. She is dressed and folding the blanket from the sofa bed.

"Mom, how are you feeling?" I ask.

"I'm fine. I want to go home. Please drive me home."

"What? Are you kidding me? You're going back there, to him? One of these days he's going to kill you."

"You're always so dramatic," Mom sighs. "I'm going home and that's that. Either you drive me or I'll walk."

I should make her walk, I think. It's two miles away and it will be a long, painful walk with her battered body.

"Fine," I say. "I'll drive you home. I just can't believe you're still putting up with his shit."

I snatch the blankets and sheets angrily and stuff them in the clothes hamper. I grab my eyeglasses and keys and stomp down the stairs and out the door without waiting for her Mom to follow. It's a beautiful spring day. The sky is deep blue and the lilac bush is in full bloom next to the back door. I breathe its scent deep into my lungs. I desperately want to separate myself from this craziness. Mom walks out the back door and presses her hand against the small of my back.

"Let's go," she orders.

We walk to the Pinto and I open her door. She still moves slowly. I close the door behind her, walk around to the driver's side and get in. We don't speak until we reach a red light two blocks away. I turn to look at my mother.

"Mom, I want you to tell me about my real dad." I'm surprised at the words coming from my mouth. "I'm 26 years old and you've been keeping this from me for ten years. I have a right to know . . . I have a right to know."

The light turns green and I look ahead and move through the intersection before turning to look at Mom again. I glance back and forth between her and the road waiting for a reaction as I try to gauge her mood. We drive several blocks before she answers.

"His name is Mike Saviano and you look just like him." Mom stares straight ahead.

Saviano, I think, *Saviano, Saviano, Saviano, Saviano. How is that spelled? Just like it sounds? S-a-v-i-a-n-o?*

"Where is he?"

"I don't know. He was in the Navy, stationed at Great Lakes naval base. I met him at a party. He doesn't know about you."

I turn this information over and over in my head. Saviano? Italian? Great Lakes naval base is in Chicago. Does that mean he is from Chicago?

We are silent as we drive the last couple of blocks. I'm not sure what to say. I have many more questions, but I know she's not going to answer them, at least not now. I pull into the driveway. Dad peers out the window at us. I throw the dirtiest look I can manage his way and get out of the car to help Mom.

Mom shrugs my arm off as I help her from the car.

"I told you, I'm fine," she says angrily. She walks toward the house and turns to look at me one last time. "Don't do anything stupid."

I know exactly what she means. She doesn't want me to look for Mike Saviano.

• • •

I start my search that afternoon.

I drive straight from Mom's house to the library and ask the reference librarian for a Chicago phonebook. There are 27 Saviano listings in the Chicago directory. I take a sheet of paper from the desk and carefully copy down every name, address and phone number. When I finish that task, I look up Great Lakes naval base and write down the main address and phone number. I fold the lined paper and stuff it in my purse.

Back at home, I begin dialing phone numbers from the list and get answering machines on my first few attempts. I'm too tongue-tied to leave messages, so I decide it's better to write to each Saviano family in Chicago. My note is simple:

> I'm trying to locate Michael Saviano who was stationed at Great Lakes naval base in 1960. I think he's approximately 45 years old. If you know him, please contact me.

I print my name, address and phone number on the bottom of each note. I address the envelopes, stamp them and drop them off at the post office on my way to get Jenny from school. I also write to Great Lakes naval base requesting the address on file for Michael Saviano.

Months crawl by without any new information on my biological father. I receive a letter from Great Lakes that says the records are closed, and they won't share any information about Mike Saviano. I get one letter from a Saviano in Chicago, which says all the Chicago Saviano families are related and the only Michael in their family is four years old. I'm at a dead end and know I will have to go back to my mother.

Bryan and I take Jenny up north for Labor Day weekend. We rent a cottage at Twin Haven Resort on North Twin Lake, which is now owned by my Mapleview friends, the Molters. My parents have a trailer down the street at the Huetten Bar resort.

Mary and I shoot pool at the Twin Haven lodge while our mothers sit at the bar. I buy Mom a couple of drinks to loosen her up. Mary knows what I'm up to, and we share a few conspiratorial laughs. After Mom and Phyllis have had a few drinks, they are as giggly as high school girls. I sit down next to Mom at the bar, balancing my pool cue between my knees.

I raise my glass. "Cheers, Mom."

"Cheers," Mom replies. She sips her drink daintily and peers at me over her glass.

"So, Mom, tell me again. Where is Mike Saviano from?"

Mom considers her glass for a long moment before she sets it back on the bar and looks me dead in the eye.

"I don't believe I ever said."

"C'mon, Mom . . . "

"Tams, what are you doing? I told you not to do anything stupid."

"It's not stupid. I don't expect you to understand," I huff. "You know who your father is."

Mom inspects her glass again, picks it up and drains it.

"He's from Boston."

"Massachusetts?" I'm surprised by this revelation.

"Yes. I have no idea where he is now. Will you please drop it?"

When I return to Milwaukee Monday evening, the first thing I do is call Boston information.

"I'm looking for a listing for Michael Saviano," I say, pen poised to write a number.

"I have a number in Woburn," the operator says.

"Okay, I'll take that." I write the number on a notepad, reconfirm it and trace over the digits one more time before I hang up the phone. I stare at the pad for a long time but am too scared to dial. This may not even be my dad, but it's my first solid lead.

I can't concentrate on anything at work the next morning. The office is quiet at lunchtime. My hand shakes as I pick up the phone and punch out the number in Boston. It may not be the right Mike Saviano, but my heart pounds and my stomach flips. A man answers on the second ring.

"Hello?"

"Ummm, hello. I'm, I'm, uh, hi, I'm looking for Michael Saviano."

"This is Mike."

"Oh, well, I'm not sure if you're the one I'm looking for . . . May I ask you a few questions?"

Short pause. "Sure."

"Ummm, were you in the Navy in 1960 stationed at Great Lakes naval base?"

"Yes."

"Yes? Oh, wow. Ummm, did you know Sandra Leavitt?"

"Yes, I know Sandra."

I feel like I'm going to faint. I haven't thought this through. What do I say now? I put my forehead down on the cool metal desk and try to breathe, to will the right words to come to me.

I choke back my tears. "I think I am your daughter."

Mike gasps on the other end of the line. We're both lost in our own emotions. Seconds pass.

My "I can't believe I found you" overlaps his "I can't believe you found me."

"You know about me?" I ask.

"Well, I couldn't be sure, but I suspected," Mike answers. "I knew your mother was pregnant, but she told me the baby wasn't mine. Part of me didn't believe her."

I tell Mike the entire story, how I found the letter when I was fifteen but didn't know his name until last spring and only two days ago learned he was from Boston. We are both a bit stunned, and although I know we have a lot to say to each other, I'm at work and my co-workers stream in the door after their lunch breaks.

"Maybe we can talk more another time?" I ask.

"I would like that," Mike says. "Give me your phone number."

We make arrangements to speak on Saturday. I hang up and brush the tears from my cheeks.

My real dad. I just talked to my real dad.

• • •

At first, Mike and I talk on the phone often. I am ready to jump right in to a relationship with my new father, but Mike is cautious. He wants to know everything about me, but shares little about his own family. I sense my existence isn't going over well with his wife. I wonder how Mike's wife feels about me, but I don't want to ask him.

Bryan is not happy that I've found Mike. He thinks it is a betrayal to my parents. We argue about it and I take it as just one more sign that Bryan is on their side. To add to my distress, Bryan and Jennifer are so close that Jenny thinks of Bryan as her father. After what she's been through with Sid, I don't want to take Bryan from her no matter how unhappy I am. I spend less and less time at home. If I'm not at work, I'm at the gym, carrying on my affair with Jack, or out with friends.

Mike and I make arrangements to meet in Boston. I check into the Holiday Inn in Woburn, and Mike comes to pick me up for lunch. He calls my room from the house phone when he arrives, and I give him my room number. I'm much too nervous to meet him in the lobby. I open the door immediately when Mike knocks. The first thing I notice is his curly hair and light eyes. *Oh my God, I do look just like him.*

Mike hugs me as if I am a delicate China doll and I squeeze him like he's my long, lost father. "You are so beautiful," he whispers in my ear, "You are so beautiful." We embrace for what seems like a long time, but I don't want to let go. We let go and step back to examine each other more closely. I can't get over how much I resemble Mike. No wonder I don't look like the rest of my family. Physically, I am all Saviano. We look so much alike that years later, my cousin Catherine, Mike's niece, nicknames Mike and I "Twinsies."

Mike and I spend a lovely day together driving around Boston and touring northern Massachusetts. He is kind, warm and funny.

I feel like I've missed out on not knowing him all these years.

When I return to Milwaukee after my visit with Mike, I start to make some changes to my life. Grandpa Ellis talks me into going back to school, and I enroll in weekend classes at Alverno College. I avoid my parents as much as possible because I don't know what to do with the anger I feel toward them for keeping Mike a secret. Once again, Bryan defends my parents and it's the last straw for me. I break up with him and ask him to move out.

The next few years pass as though I am on autopilot. I work full time, attend classes as a communications major at Alverno every other weekend and try to raise my daughter in a calm and peaceful environment. My affair with Jack ends and I cling to my girlfriend Marilyn, who is going through her own struggles. Marilyn and I spend the last years of our 20s together as young, single women on the town. Marilyn is my new lifeline. We go to concerts and summer festivals and nightclubs and bars—futilely looking for good men and searching for ourselves.

Although I keep my distance from my parents, I am at the hospital when Dad goes through his second round of open-heart surgery in 1989. This time, the surgery almost kills him. Rick and I flank Mom in the waiting room when the surgeon comes out to speak with her.

"It's bad," he says. "I can't get his heart to start pumping again. We're doing all we can, but I'm not sure he's going to make it."

Mom wilts into Rick's arms. Part of me is terrified he is going to die. Another part of me believes my dad is too ornery to go without a fight. If only the good die young, he should be here for a while.

Meeting Mike Saviano, my biological father, for the first time, 1988.

CHAPTER 13

Some Things You're Born To, Some Things You Better Learn

It is Patrick Dean who finally saves me. Well, not literally. The thought of killing myself had never crossed my mind, and he didn't pull me from the path of a speeding car or anything like that. Perhaps I shouldn't sound so dramatic about it. But when I recall my life back then, there is no doubt in my mind that things would be different if not for Patrick's intervention.

It's fair to say that I am totally numb by the time Patrick walks into my life in 1991. Although Dad survived his heart surgery, both my great-grandmothers Bessie and Gert died the previous year, and I struggle to come to grips with the growing pile of losses. I feel detached. Indifferent. Unmoved. About everything. If pain or pleasure tries to creep into my psyche, I quickly dull the feelings with copious amounts of wine or logging miles on the lake trail. On some subconscious level I do not want to feel anything.

Patrick comes into my office on a relentlessly cold Monday in January. By this time, thanks to my classes at Alverno and my grandpa's persistence, I have what many people consider a great job managing a high-end executive business center. Our shared-office suites are located on the third floor of an ultra-modern building in an office park in the affluent Milwaukee suburb of Brookfield. One full side of the building is windows. On this wintry morning an icy wind whips and whistles against the glass and even the inside walls are bitten with frost. A space heater buzzes under the desk in my elegant private office. My feet, covered only in lightweight pumps, are always cold.

The receptionist pokes her head around my door. "There's someone here to see you about an office."

I glance at my date book.

"He doesn't have an appointment but said you sent him a letter?"

Ah. That stupid marketing letter. Our national office is in the middle of a big marketing campaign, which includes sending letters to businesses in the immediate area inviting them to look at our space. Irritated, I check myself in a compact mirror and attempt to pat down my unruly curls. I smear gloss on my dry lips, adjust the pantyhose that choke the circulation from my legs and force a smile before I walk to the reception area.

Patrick is turned away from me gazing out the conference room window at the bleak sky and gray snow and ice. From the back, he doesn't look like he belongs in the polished, corporate setting. For one thing, he doesn't seem to be in any hurry, which is quite different from the other executives who lease office space here. And he is dressed casually—no expensive Italian business suit for this guy. Patrick's hands are stuffed into the pockets of an insulated jacket worn over casual khaki slacks.

"Dreary weather, huh?" I say to get his attention.

He turns to me and extends his hand. "Any day out of a hospital is a good day."

I find the remark odd but don't comment on it.

Patrick wears his dark hair on the long-ish side and sports a full beard and mustache, another sign that he is not a typical executive. I guess he's about 35. He seems like a serious guy. His smile is warmer than most, and he doesn't launch into the over-the-top salesman swagger I have come to despise. Patrick is altogether different.

Patrick did receive the marketing letter from our corporate office. He tells me he has no intention of moving from his current office down the street, but at the last minute a client had canceled and Patrick decided to come over to kill some time.

"What do you do?" I ask as I lead him down the hallway.

"I'm a grief counselor."

This catches me off guard. Again, I make no comment. My other clients are sales people in manufacturing, insurance, pharmaceuticals, electronics. Grief counselor? What exactly does a grief counselor do?

The suites are newly renovated, and I show Patrick the amenities as we head toward the vacant office. My heels click on the gleaming tiled floors as Patrick—hands still in his pockets—looks up, down and around taking in the skylights, the solid oak planters brimming with greenery and the contemporary artwork hanging on freshly painted teal and gray walls.

The vacant office is at the back of the building overlooking a nature preserve. I unlock the door and open it wide. The oversized window frames a graceful doe and her freckled fawn standing in the snow at the edge of the woods. Perfect staging. Patrick stands quietly at the window watching the deer for several minutes. He signs a one-year lease before the week is out.

The next time I see Patrick is moving day. I stop at his door to say hello and chat with him for a few minutes while he unpacks boxes. I ask him how he spends his time as a grief counselor. Patrick explains. He says that although the death of a loved one is a loss, grief affects people with many other losses—what he calls "little deaths." I have no idea what he means, but it makes me uncomfortable. I change the subject back to something safe and then excuse myself.

Patrick settles in easily and after a week it seems like he has been there forever. He is immediately popular with my staff and the other tenants. He has more visitors than any of us. Most mornings Patrick stops at my office door to say hello or to introduce me to his guests. One day he introduces me to his friend Jody.

"Your eyes are so beautiful!" Jody exclaims as she shakes my hand. "I've never seen eyes so blue."

I feel my face flush. "Oh, well . . . they're so big it's like I have fish eyes."

"Fish eyes!?" Patrick laughs, but it isn't a cruel laugh. He seems surprised, like he can't believe I said that.

Tingling with embarrassment, I excuse myself to make a phone call.

On my thirtieth birthday, Patrick slips a card under my office door. The cover shot is an original photograph of a vase of roses. Inside the card he had written: "I'm glad you were born." His sweetness stirs something inside of me. I am not accustomed to random acts of kindness. Feeling rather shy, I ask Patrick to lunch to thank him for renting the office.

We go down the street to a little café, and over spinach quiche Patrick asks me questions about my life. I deflect, make jokes, try to keep things light.

"I think you're an unhappy person," Patrick says directly. He leans back in his chair and sips his Coke from a straw. He seems to be waiting for me to respond. Okay. Now I'm angry. I feel my face blush—again. Who the hell is this guy to judge me and tell me I'm unhappy? I try to keep my composure in front of him, but I'm rattled. My appetite is gone. I don't want to be in the same room with Patrick, but I am stuck. For the rest of our lunch I make uncomfortable small talk.

I avoid Patrick for several days. I close my office door when I hear him greet the receptionist each morning so he can't stop to say hello. His comment hurts, as truth often does, and I don't know what to do with it. For days, it eats away at me. Patrick pokes his head into my office the first morning I leave the door open.

"Mornin'. How are you?"

"Patrick, may I speak with you privately when it's convenient?" *I sound like a screech owl*, I think to myself.

"Sure, give me about 10 minutes and come on down to my office. We can look at the deer."

I spend a few minutes gathering my courage. This man exasperates me, but I don't know why. I march down the hall to Patrick's office for the first time, determined to keep a tight lid on my emotions. Predictably, Patrick's office is decorated differently from the other clients. Soft lamps replace the harsh florescent ceiling fixtures. Patrick's own nature photography, beautifully framed, hangs on the walls. A sturdy desk, comfortable chairs and a sofa give the office a homey feel. Music plays softly in the background. I take it all in for a moment. Maybe I even relax a little.

"Have a seat wherever you'd like," Patrick says.

"I prefer to stand." I do not want to be in a position of weakness with him.

"Okaaayyyy . . ." Patrick is clearly amused by my tone, and it annoys the hell out of me. I fold my arms in front of me. "Patrick, why do you think I'm an unhappy person? What leads you to believe that?" Even to my own ears I sound defensive.

He comes around from behind his desk to stand in front of me. The old *Saturday Night Live* skit "come closer, move away" pops into my head as Patrick puts his hand on my shoulder and looks directly into my eyes.

"You seem unhappy to me for many reasons. You joke about

things that aren't funny, things that are actually heartbreaking. You make self-deprecating comments about yourself, and you won't accept a compliment, no matter how small. You have a real sadness in your eyes and the way you carry yourself. I deal with many people in pain and I see that you're hurting."

Once again, I have no clue how to respond. No one has ever said these kinds of things to me. There is a long silence between us while I try to come up with something—anything—to stuff this genie back in the bottle.

Patrick breaks the silence. "If you ever want to talk with me about anything, I'm here."

"Uhhhh . . . thanks. I better get back to work." I leave Patrick's office shaking.

How dare he? He doesn't know me. He doesn't know anything about me. I tick off a list in my head: I have a good job, a beautiful daughter, friends, Mom and my grandparents. Sure, Dad is a handful, but other than that I am doing fine, the best I can. I make it back to my office, close the door and sink into the safety of my chair.

Clearly, I am not fine.

Patrick's words are under my skin like a trapped insect burring itself into my flesh. As I doodle on my desk pad, I feel fear—like poisonous venom spreading from my stomach to my legs, weakening my limbs and working its way back up my body, stopping to thump my chest before reaching a full-tilt buzz in my head. I throw my pen across the desk and lean over and retch into the wastebasket.

• • •

About a month after my conversation with Patrick, I need a grief counselor. My grandpa Ellis, the one man in my life I love and trust beyond measure, is diagnosed with cancer. There is little chance he'll live much longer.

I take Patrick up on his offer to talk. As much as I do not want to discuss the probability of my grandpa's death, on top of the recent deaths of my great-grandmothers, I think I might die first if someone doesn't help me. Life without Gramps is unimaginable.

I watch a succession of people go in and out of Patrick's office. They all look like reasonably intelligent folks, and if they talk to Patrick about their problems . . . well, I try to convince myself it's okay for me to talk to him. Still terrified, I make an appointment to see Patrick on a Wednesday afternoon. He asks me to schedule two hours with him. I think that's excessive but decide I can bail out early if it doesn't go well.

I show up at Patrick's door promptly for our first meeting. He invites me to sit down and I choose one of the comfortable chairs. I am definitely not interested in, God forbid, lying on the sofa. He gives me a few minutes to relax by making small talk about the deer living in the woods outside his window and tells me about his home on the Fox River. I am reluctant to bring up my grandfather right away.

"How do you usually start with someone new?" I ask Patrick.

"Is there anything specific you want to talk about?"

"No."

"Well, tell me about your family. What are your parents like? How many brothers and sisters do you have?"

Oh, Christ. The last thing I want to discuss is my family. I give Patrick just the facts. My Dad is a retired car salesman with heart problems. Mom works in a factory. I have three younger brothers. I'm close to my youngest, Rick, but don't see much of the other two.

Patrick asks probing questions about my childhood, and I try to brush him off with quick answers, no real depth. At first he is patient with me, nodding his head as if he understands, not pressing for more than I am willing to give.

"Tell me about Christmas when you were seven years old," Patrick says.

"I don't remember that far back."

"Sure you do." Patrick pushes me. "What grade were you in? Who was your teacher? Who was your best friend? What did you do for fun?"

Patrick forces me to remember things better left behind.

• • •

I recount several stories from my life to Patrick during our first session, and I am exhausted when I leave his office. Overwhelming emotions well up inside me. I can't breathe and feel like there is no oxygen in the hallway between Patrick's office and mine. I stop long enough to grab my purse and car keys and then bolt down three flights of stairs and out the door. Gulping fresh air, I manage to hold back the tears until I shut the car door behind me. In the safety of my leather seat I grasp the steering wheel and break down. I stay in the parking lot for a good twenty minutes before I'm able to pull myself together enough to drive. Tears flow down my cheeks soaking my neck and the collar of my blouse as I make the half hour commute home.

I cry long into the night and fall into a deep sleep with dark dreams of choking on something full and sticky—like putty in my mouth and throat. When I crawl out of bed the following morning, my body feels heavy and drugged. I cannot stop crying. I call in sick because I can't seem to get a grip. I am completely burned out and afraid, yet there is something else, long buried inside me, beginning to surface. For the first time in a long time, a sliver of hope shines through the darkness.

• • •

Therapy is excruciating. Patrick pushes me to relive every painful moment of my past and then reexamine it from the perspective of a thirty-year-old woman. I come to realize how much anger I've suppressed over the years. Anger at my parents, yes, but also anger at myself for who I had not become, for walking through my own life unaware and indifferent, parenting my daughter half-heartedly, choosing to spend time with men who belittle me, use me or ignore me. I have been playing the role of the wild party girl for years although truthfully it has never suited me.

I have no passion or aspirations for my life and my jobs were only a means to an end—paying the rent.

"When you were a little girl, what did you want to be when you grew up?" Patrick asks me one afternoon. The April rain pours down outside, drenching the newly greened forest. I take a moment to listen to it pelt against the window. An occasional lightening flash crosses the shadow of Patrick's face as he sits quietly waiting for me to speak.

"A writer," I confess. "Isn't that silly? My cousins Lori and Tracy and I always had this grand plan that when we grew up we would share an apartment. They were going to be hairdressers and I was going to be a writer."

"What would you write?" Patrick asks.

"I don't know."

"C'mon," Patrick prods. "What did you dream about writing?"

"Well, I always thought I'd write for *Rolling Stone*. I wanted to write about music. And I did think about writing books."

The next time we meet, Patrick brings me a copy of John Irving's *A Prayer for Owen Meany* and a thin book called *How to Write and Sell*. I think it is a nice gesture, but reading a "how-to" book isn't going to turn me into John Irving. Patrick senses my hesitation.

"You're already a writer, you know."

"I am?"

"Sure, you've been keeping a journal since junior high, that's a lot of years of writing."

"That doesn't count," I brush him off. "It's not creative. I'm not creative."

Patrick throws his head back and gales of deep laughter bounce off the windows and walls. He wipes the moisture from his eyes and gasps for air as he tries to regain control.

"You're hilarious," I giggle. "What is so funny?"

"I'm not creative," Patrick mimics my voice. "That's a good one."

• • •

As my sessions with Patrick continue, I begin to feel strong and independent. In my grief over Grandpa's illness, coupled with the childhood stories I share with Patrick, I feel even more anger toward my dad and, surprisingly, my mom.

The last good time I had with Dad was the previous autumn. Dad had come to see the office suites shortly after the renovation was complete. As we walk around the building, I introduce him to my tenants. Each of them says a kind word about me and Dad beams. "That's my Penelope," he says. He strolls through the offices with his arm around my shoulder singing "The Most Beautiful Girl."

Dad ruins that memory a mere week after his visit when there is a write up about our new offices and my position as general manager in the *Milwaukee Business Journal*.

When I show Mom and Dad the magazine, Dad is drunk. I show him the article and he crumples the paper, throws it at my feet and sneers: "Who did you have to sleep with to get that written?"

• • •

I share our biggest family secret with Patrick—that my dad is not my real dad—and above everything else, I am most angry that they kept the truth from me about Mike Saviano for so many years. As I try to work through my demons, I remember only the bad times and can't make room for the possibility that my life at home was ever anything but horrible. I blame my parents for everything that ever went wrong. Now Grandpa is dying and someone has to pay.

Patrick suggests I write letters to each of my parents telling them how I feel. "You don't have to mail them," Patrick says, "but this will give you a chance to say what you want to say—to get it down on paper."

I write the letters. In part the letter to my dad says:

> I'm going to say some things to you I have never said before. First of all, I want to tell you why I haven't spent much time with you and Mom over the past several years. This may hurt you, but I have not wanted to see you because I have been angry and hurt. When I was a little girl, you were an alcoholic. You were verbally and physically abusive to my mother, my brothers and me.
>
> Sometimes you would come home drunk and fight with Mom. I would sneak into my brothers' room and take Ricky into my bedroom with me. Because he was the baby, I was always worried that he would die. I thought he was the most helpless one and that I could pick him up and run away fast from you if you attacked us . . . I remember you taking us to the circus. You got the tickets from some Shriner friends and wanted Robbie and me to go up to them and thank them. We wouldn't do it because we were shy. At that

point in my life, I was afraid of everything. The hats the Shriners wore scared me . . . because we wouldn't thank your friends, you got drunk, you called us ungrateful, you said we made your life miserable. You drove like a maniac on the way home the car spun out of control in the rain. I thought I was going to die. I was a child. I was innocent.

I thought that parents knew everything. I thought it was my fault when you were mean . . . When I was 15 and we moved into our new house, I found a box of letters that you and Mom wrote to each other when you were in the Army . . . the content of those letters told me that I was not your daughter. I was angry, sad, and relieved all at the same time. Angry because you and Mom kept it a secret, sad because I felt like I didn't belong to anyone, and relieved because I hated you and felt released from your power.

After it was out of the bag that I wasn't your daughter, you took many opportunities to tell me I was a slut like my mother and that I was not your daughter . . . you were always drunk. You spent every night either in the garage or the basement with your bottle of brandy and your music cranked up so the entire neighborhood could hear it. It didn't matter that your children were trying to study or sleep.

I remember one night you woke me up after midnight on a school night to make me scrub the kitchen floor. I remember you throwing water on me to get me up some mornings. You thought it was a joke. The abuse didn't magically stop when I moved out like I thought it would. You have manipulated me through my adult life, too, telling me if I didn't listen to you I would never get any help from you. Anytime I have been successful at a job you would tell me I was going to get fired. You always told me that no man would ever want me. You've always told me I was a terrible mother . . . you've tried to punish me for behavior you find unacceptable.

I should not go out and leave my daughter with a sitter, I should not hang around with men, I should not talk to people you don't like, I should not tell anyone about our family secrets.

All of the abuse I have endured has negatively affected my life. Until recently, I was a terribly damaged person. I've been involved with needy, dysfunctional men because I thought I could take care of them and change them. I've had a deplorable lack of belief in myself, in my ability and in my worthiness. That is why I am such an overachiever. I'm continually trying to be perfect. I was afraid to sit back and relax because I was always told I was lazy.

I could never accept love from anyone. When someone would express love for me, I thought they had ulterior motives. I have a negative self-image about my body because you always told me I was fat. I never believed I could make it through college because you always told me I was stupid.

This is what I want from you if you're interested in establishing a healthy relationship with me. I want you to apologize for being such a cruel, lousy father. I want you to acknowledge that the harm you did to me caused me much pain and sadness. I want you to stop the verbal attacks . . . I would like you to acknowledge that good fathers do not insult or degrade their daughters. I have tolerated that from you in the past but I will not tolerate it anymore . . . I want you to acknowledge that my life is mine and that you do not have any authority over me.

Dad, I don't know you very well. I don't know what pain and fear and sadness you have been through in your life . . . I'm grateful that you were a hard worker and a good provider. I'm glad we had nice things and a place up north. I remember the times when you were sober and you laughed and joked around a lot . . . I remember how scared you were when you got sick, I remember how sad you were when your parents died. I'm sorry that you and I didn't have the relationship we could have had. I missed a lot by not being able to give my love to a father I so wanted to love . . .

Impulsively, I mail the letters. Part of me is sorry the minute I hear the whoosh of the envelopes disappear into the black hole of the mailbox. The angry part of me thinks it serves them right. They should know what they've done to me. I don't consider the fact that my mom's father is dying and she has enough stress to deal with at this point.

"You mailed the letters?" Patrick is surprised. "Okayyyyy. . . ."

Thankfully, Patrick doesn't dwell on the potential consequences, but I find out soon enough when my brother Rick calls me. Without preamble he asks: "What did you do?"

"What are you talking about?" I ask.

How could you write those letters to Mom and Dad? Especially now when Grandpa is dying?"

I feel a momentary pang of guilt. I would never do anything to intentionally hurt my grandparents. *This has nothing to do with them*, I think. *This is between my parents and me.* I push the guilt aside and feel only anger.

"What about what Dad has done to me, to all of us?"

"You exaggerate," Rick replies. "You never remember the good, only the bad."

"Now you sound like Mom," I say.

"He's never going to forgive you for this one," Rick says.

"Well, maybe I'm not going to forgive him."

With my grandparents (Ellis and Jeanne Leavitt) shortly before my grand-father's death in 1991.

CHAPTER 14

Better Days

During therapy with Patrick, I decide to change my last name to Saviano. The name Ruditys has been a curse since my grade school days.

Many classmates' parents warned their kids to stay away from me because of the trouble my name suggested. Two generations of Ruditys bad boys had left their mark on the town of St. Francis. This was probably a badge of honor for my brothers. Having the name Ruditys meant no one would mess with them. But for me, perhaps because I'm a girl, it was painful. I walked around Willow Glen Elementary School trying to remain invisible. I felt embarrassed and sad whenever someone ridiculed the Ruditys name—and it happened often.

During my time with Patrick, the Ruditys name again gains negative attention as my dad's brother, Joe, former Milwaukee Firefighters Union president, is gunning for the job of assistant fire chief. Many in Milwaukee oppose his appointment and in true Ruditys fashion, Uncle Joe yanks the gloves off and fights his battle in the media. Each night, I find my *Milwaukee Journal* on the front porch with headlines blaring: RUDITYS PROMOTION ILLEGAL, CITY ATTORNEYS SAY; CALLERS SPEAK OUT ON RUDITYS; GIVE RUDITYS SELECTION A HARD LOOK; SEELEN'S NOMINEE

FACES TOUGH FIGHT FOR NO. 2 JOB; 'DISCUSSION' AT FIRE PICNIC GOT HOT.

The headlines are the topic of conversation at work, at the gym, at the bar, and, with all due respect to my uncle Joe and his career aspirations, I just want to banish the Ruditys name from my life so I can remain invisible.

At first, because of my close relationship with my grandparents, I think about changing my name to Mom's maiden name of Leavitt. But, the more I think about it, the more I want my biological father's name—the name I had been denied when Mom made the choice to marry Bob Ruditys.

"What do you think?" I ask Patrick.

He throws it back at me: "The important question is what do you think? Have you thought about living with the name? Have you thought about how it will change you? Do you feel like it would be a good change?"

"Yes, I do." I am excited about taking my dad's name. Although I am asking Patrick for his opinion I've already made up my mind.

When I tell Mike I plan to change my last name to Saviano, he tries to talk me out of it.

"It's not that I don't want you to have my name," he says. "I just worry that you'll hurt your mother."

I do not waver. "This isn't your decision," I tell Mike. "My last name should have been Saviano all along."

• • •

Changing my name is the third strike that finally ruins my relationship with my dad for good. Although we had been heading in that direction for years, the chain reaction that finally breaks us starts in that early summer of 1991.

Shortly before I write the kiss-off letters to my parents (which is Strike Two) I walk into Venus Ford and purchase a Bronco II without my dad's help. (Strike One.) Although I am thirty years old, my dad has helped me get every car I've ever owned.

The day after I buy it, I park the Bronco in front of my brother Steve's house when I show up for a birthday party for my nephew. Dad watches from the front lawn as I hop down from the driver's seat. I take my time as I reach back into the Bronco for my purse. Before I extract myself, I lift my Converse gym shoe back up on the running board to tie the laces. Dad stares at me and doesn't say a word until I close the door and turn around.

"Whose car is that?" Dad's face is red.

Unlike past history between us, I don't hesitate or worry about his reaction. I look Dad in the eye and feel a twinge of pleasure even though I am well aware this will hurt him. "It's mine."

"You ungrateful bitch!" he screams. "You did this just to spite me."

I shrug. This time the statement has more than a kernel of truth to it.

Within two months time, I have purchased a car without my dad's help, written antagonistic letters to both my parents and unapologetically changed my name to Saviano. I'm not fazed when Rick tells me that our parents officially disown me.

I continue therapy with Patrick and sign up for the summer class on death and dying he teaches at Cardinal Stritch College. As my education with Patrick progresses, so does my Grandpa's cancer. I spend as much time with Gramps as possible. As a younger man, Grandpa looked like Jimmy Stewart in *It's a Wonderful Life* or *The Philadelphia Story*. He's lanky and loose-limbed with tousled hair and a mischievous grin. I wonder if Grandpa still thinks of himself as that younger man.

Although he doesn't physically resemble the actor by the time I know him (Grandpa wears his hair in a crew cut even before the chemo makes him lose it), his personality still seems similar. Like many of Stewart's characters, Grandpa is playful—an affection tease—enchanted with his six daughters and flock of grandchildren. He is a family man, hard worker, honorable, honest, warm and gracious.

I have my grandpa's eyes. Sometimes when I look in the mirror and see those eyes staring back at me, I am at peace about him always being part of me. Our eyes are the bluest blue, somewhere between the colors of the sky and the sea. Only three percent of the world population has blue eyes, so it's no wonder that even strangers regularly comment on mine.

During this time when my grandpa is dying, my mom and her sisters are always at Grandma and Grandpa's house. My mom has five sisters and all six of them are strong, opinionated women. They are known simply as "The Sisters" in our family, almost as if they were interchangeable. The Sisters remind me of Russian nesting dolls—each forming a protective cover over each other. When I was a kid, I accepted their closeness easily and assumed all sisters were like The Sisters. It wasn't until I experienced other family dynamics that I realized the especially intimate relationship my mother and aunts share.

While Grandpa is sick, my grandparents' house buzzes with activity late into the evenings. Grandpa is confined to a hospital bed in the guest room and he has hospice care. We all know it's getting close to the end. His condition declines significantly in the weeks after my final falling out with my parents.

I continue to spend time at the house, surrounded by aunts, uncles and cousins. It's awkward with Mom and we ignore each other, buffered between other family members. It's obvious to me that The Sisters know what's going on, and I feel the anger directed at me. Grandma is too worried about Grandpa to say much, although she pulls me aside in the kitchen to hug me and tell me that she loves me. "This will pass," Grandma reassures me.

On August 29, Grandpa is taken from hospice care at home to Trinity Memorial Hospital. I join my family for the vigil at his bedside. Because I am at the hospital day and night, my dad refuses to be there, although it's clear my mom needs him.

"Why don't you go home so Dad will come up here?" Rick asks me.

"I'm not stopping him," I say.

"He won't come as long as you're here."

"That's his problem. I'm not leaving Grandpa."

Grandpa dies in the early morning hours of August 31, 1991. The family is gathered around his bed as his breathing slows and he slips into a coma. I hold his hand. When Grandma realizes death is imminent she cries out to Grandpa: "Ellis, please don't go. Don't leave." It seems like Grandpa hears her and struggles for air.

"Mom, you have to let him go," my aunts say, circling around their mother and whispering words of comfort.

"Okay, Ellis, it's okay," Grandma leans down to kiss her husband of 53 years. "I love you."

With that, Grandpa takes his last quiet breath and is still. Grandma hangs her head over him and cries. My aunts turn to their husbands for comfort. My mother stands alone hugging her arms around her waist. I catch her eye and feel her anger. I am a pariah. The pain in my heart is unbearable and I am utterly alone.

The funeral director shows up to take Grandpa's body and my family walks together down the hallway toward the exit. I trail behind them carrying a pile of Grandpa's clothing and his shoes. I bury my face into Grandpa's shirt, breathe in his scent and cry.

My cousins and I hold each other together over the next few days. Grandma is deep in the throes of grief, and Mom and her sisters build a silent blockade around her. None of them speaks to me. Still, I refuse to leave my grandma's house and spend most of my time on the front porch with my cousins. My dad never comes to the house, but he does finally show up at church for the funeral. We avoid each other. The one time our eyes meet across the room, I sense his rage and know better than to approach him.

Patrick comes to the wake to show his support. I'm grateful to see his friendly face and we fall into an easy embrace. I take Patrick's hand and lead him to Grandpa's casket.

We talk for a few moments.

"You were lucky to have each other," Patrick says.

I nod, too choked up to talk.

After Patrick leaves, my brother Rick grabs my arm and angrily pulls me outside. "Who was that?"

"Patrick, my grief counselor."

"How could you let him come here? He's the one who put all these shitty ideas in your head about Dad."

"Rick, no one put anything in my head about Dad. It seems like the rest of you have selective memories and can't face the truth."

Rick shakes his head and walks away.

• • •

By the time my thirtieth year comes to an end, my life has turned 180 degrees within a year. Grandpa is dead. My parents have disowned me. I have a new job. And, yes, I have another new boyfriend.

Shortly after Grandpa's death, I begin dating Jim Kotarak. Jim's younger brother Jerry and I had been pals since high school, and Jerry is also my friend Marilyn's boyfriend. Jim is a bodybuilder, a former Mr. Wisconsin. He is into fitness and I turn him on to the joy of running. We compete in 5k, 10k and half-marathon races nearly every weekend and that is our primary bond. Jim is also divorced with three great kids, and I devote myself to Jill, Jason and JJ. I feel like I have a new family.

The entire Kotarak family welcomes Jenny and me with open hearts. In the absence of my own family, they are loving surrogates. The months are now marked with Kotarak family rituals: birthday parties, dinners at the Moose Lodge and events at the K-Ranch tavern—the family business Jerry and Marilyn will eventually take over.

Jim loves country music and listens to the local country station, WMIL. Radio doesn't play the likes of Johnny Cash and Willie Nelson anymore, and I'm grateful that this new music does not remind me of Dad. In 1991, country music is on top thanks to the incredible success of Garth Brooks.

One night Jim and Marilyn coax Jerry and me into seeing a new artist, Collin Raye, in concert. Collin's hit song, "Love, Me" captivates me as it stirs memories of Grandpa, and Collin's show is my introduction to this strange new world of honky-tonks and modern country music. Even in Milwaukee, fans dress in western shirts and cowboy boots, and line dancing is so popular that country nightclubs spring up all over the city.

Partly because of Jim's love of country music, I apply for an internship at Sundance Broadcasting, which owns WMIL and WOKY radio stations. The radio business is different than anything I've experienced, and I fall in love with it. After a semester of interning in the promotion department, I stay on to work for the stations full time. It's fun work. Our FM country station leads ratings nearly every book. Our AM station wins honors for being the "good news" stop on the dial. Sundance's mission statement is that "The Most Fun Wins," and they mean it.

Our leaders are president Mike Jorgenson and general manager Brian Ongaro. They're driven as much by the excitement and fun as they are by the bottom line and are living examples of the adage: "Do what you love and the money will follow." To this day, Brian and Mike are the most influential business mentors of my career.

I can't believe this is my life now. I work with an imaginative, accomplished and creative group of people during one of the most exciting times in Milwaukee radio. The environment is both relaxed and stimulating. Laughter rings out from every corner of the building. We all like each other at Sundance and the sense of camaraderie is extraordinary. Naturally, there is friendly competition in the sales department, but everyone works together with the shared goal of building WMIL and WOKY into the best radio stations in Milwaukee.

Jenny is in junior high, and I have more freedom to work and have a social life. I'm the director of database marketing at the station, which includes editing and publishing WMIL's *Country Today* and WOKY's *The Best of Times* magazines. Our marketing director, Jerry Arndt, teaches me everything he knows about creating a magazine. I'm green as can be, yet I am the writer, editor, photographer and art director. We hire a team of desktop publishers to design the magazine, and I spend hours poring over layouts and designs, choosing photos and writing tag lines.

In the weeks leading up to my printing deadlines, I pull several all-nighters at the station and many times the only other person in the building is our overnight jock. I'm so excited on press days that I am up and out of the house by 5:30 a.m. to drive the 40 miles to the printer to watch my magazine come off the web press.

Our program director, Kerry Wolfe, and our music director, Mitch Morgan, tutor me on everything I want to know about country music and its history. They introduce me to the executives at record labels in Nashville to help me land interviews with artists for the magazine, and I make friends with colleagues who work on Music Row.

Considering my dad's record collection, it is no surprise I am drawn to traditional country music and its weeping steel guitars, twin fiddles and rural themes. I am a fan of Americana music before there is a word for it, and I fall in love with the music of Lyle Lovett, Rosanne Cash, Rodney Crowell, Guy Clark, Townes Van Zandt, Emmylou Harris, Kris Kristofferson, Dwight Yoakam and Mary Chapin Carpenter.

All of us "Sundancers" are a close-knit bunch and even when I'm not working, I spend most of my free time with my colleagues. We women share a particularly special bond.

The years at Sundance and the break from my family give me a fresh start and a new perspective. I embrace life. I open myself to grand possibilities. I try to shed negative thinking. I use the magazines as my creative outlet. I build strong relationships with people who do not know, or care, about my past. And, most of all, I surround myself with music.

Mike Saviano visits often and our relationship grows closer. I meet the extended Saviano family. Although I was not raised as a Saviano, it becomes clear as soon as I get to know them that our blood ties and shared Italian lineage is as powerful and necessary as the connective tissue in my own body. Mike's sister Corinne becomes more like a second mother to me than an aunt. I am so much like Corinne—we are both emotional, candid and tend to over share our feelings. Corinne's daughter Catherine is warm and grounded—the sister I always wanted. I am attached to the Saviano clan by an invisible, safe and strong umbilical cord—a foundation of love that feeds my confidence. I feel like I can accomplish anything.

Part of my job is to manage the WMIL "country club." Listeners who join the free club receive a free subscription to the magazine.

It's a way for the station to build its database of listeners and establish a relationship with them.

Because I feel emotionally stronger, I believe it might be a good time to make amends with my dad. As a peace offering, I enter Dad's information into our database shortly before his birthday in May. I mail him a birthday card along with the red plastic membership card and a copy of the magazine. Less than a week later, I find an envelope in my stack of mail with familiar handwriting. There is no return address, but I know his scrawl. My heart races as I rip open the envelope. Dad's membership card is cut into four pieces; the birthday card and the magazine are torn in half inside the envelope. I empty the envelope on my desk and search through the contents. There is no note, no other form of correspondence. He still knows how to be cruel. This is his official "fuck you."

You bastard, I think. The room tilts as I reach back to grab the arm of my chair. I lower my shaking body into the seat and breathe deeply as I try to contain the swirling emotions of anger, disappointment and hurt. I push the broken pieces from the envelope to the front of my desk and swipe them into the trash.

I need a moment to myself from the office I share with Mitch, so I walk toward the ladies room and wave at the jocks through studio windows as I pass them. Breathe. Breathe. Breathe. I wait until I am safe in the stall before I let the tears fall. Why does this still hurt so much? I cry for a few minutes and then banish my sadness. This is my new life without Dad. *I don't need him*, I think. *I don't need this drama.*

• • •

Life at Sundance allows me so many new opportunities for growth and, bit-by-bit, it changes my relationship with Jim Kotarak.

He's a great guy who I will love forever, but our philosophical differences about life are too much for me to overcome. I am coming into my own for the first time, and I long to be with people who think and believe like I do. We break up.

In 1995, after a particularly long and cold winter, during one of our late-night breakfasts at Ma Fischer's diner, Raul Malo talks me into moving to Nashville.

By this time, Raul and I had been friends for a couple of years. I met Raul when his band, The Mavericks, played a show at Chicago's Whiskey River nightclub.

"What would I do in Nashville?" I ask.

"Anything you want," Raul says. "You're creative, smart and driven. Nashville is a Mecca for people like you. I think you'd love it."

Charlie Rich dies a week before Jenny and I move to Nashville. I know he is dead when I turn on my car radio and hear the opening melody for "The Most Beautiful Girl." In 1995, (as it still is now, sadly) country radio only plays classic songs on the occasion of the artist's death. I sing along softly as memories flood through me—my dad's smile, the way he laughs at me when I resist his efforts to get me to dance with him to this song, and how he sings to me when he is trying to make up.

For a brief moment, I think about driving to my parents' house to try to force Dad to talk to me. It's been four years since we've seen or spoken to each other. I want him to hug me like he did when I was his baby girl. I want to put this silly feud behind us. I sing along with the final chorus longing for my daddy.

Mitch announces the song and confirms my suspicion. Charlie Rich is dead. I pick up my car phone and call the radio station hotline to find out how he died. I resist the temptation to call Dad. That relationship is over.

Moving to Nashville, August 1, 1995.

CHAPTER 15

Nashville

Music Row in the 1990s is like a busy college campus. Thanks to the mega-success of Garth Brooks and Shania Twain, business is booming and country is the biggest music of the day. Record label rosters are deep with artists and studios flourish. Country radio play lists are long, which means there are more opportunities for songwriters to get their songs recorded. And, there is plenty of media to cover country music.

For me, real life in Nashville is better than any fantasy. I immerse myself in my new life in the music business. I work in artist management briefly, then move on to a job in promotions at Capitol Records, then back to the media world as a writer at *Country Weekly*, then an editor at *Country Music* magazine, and a producer at Great American Country cable network before I finally I start my own media company.

Meanwhile, I meet people from all over the country who have come here for the same reason. Hardly anyone in the music business is from Nashville, and because we live away from family and home, we form a strong community.

Jenny, too, flourishes in Nashville. As a student at Hillsboro High School she auditions and is accepted in the SophistiCats show choir, the centerpiece of her teenage years in Music City. She spends her weekends at Bongo Java, a coffee shop hangout for young artists and musicians.

Shortly after I move to Nashville, I meet a guy from Wisconsin. He's cute, he's in a band and mostly because of our shared background and love of music, Karl and I fall into a relationship that is equal parts friendship and convenience with just enough romance and sex to keep me from searching for something more meaningful.

Even in Nashville, there remain constant reminders of my dad and his music. While working as a music journalist, I interview Johnny Cash for a magazine feature and attend a press party at the Cash house when June Carter hosts a CD release party. I report a story with Hank Williams Jr. at his home in Paris, Tennessee, and spend time on Willie Nelson's smoked-filled tour bus as he talks about Texas music. I write Tammy Wynette's obituary, cover Loretta Lynn at the Opry and talk to Dolly Parton about her own father.

I still go back to Wisconsin often to visit Grandma Jeanne and my brother Rick, who has been sober for years, married Kim and now has three children. But it isn't until six years after my move to Music City that I see my dad for the first time in a decade.

It is a sunny July morning in 2001, and I'm with Gram eating breakfast in a café on Packard Avenue in Cudahy when Dad walks in. We haven't spoken to each other in ten years. Gram and her friend Bill sit across from me in a booth—I face the door and they face the back of the restaurant. I see Dad walk in the front door, but he doesn't notice me. A chorus of "Hey Bobby!" greets his arrival and as usual he is the center of attention from the moment he enters the place.

Dad plays his part like he's the mayor, slapping men on the backs, shaking hands, kissing cheeks. I smile as I watch the scene unfold. It has been many years, but this is still the dad of my youth—genuinely happy to be surrounded by folks he's known through the years, friends he's helped with car repairs and purchases, people he's introduced to each other. Long before Malcolm Gladwell wrote *The Tipping Point*, my dad was a connector. He always knows someone who knows someone who can help.

He's so busy joking with his comrades that Dad doesn't spot Gram, Bill and me eating scrambled eggs in the scarred, wooden booth. It isn't until he makes his way to the back of the restaurant and takes a seat several booths behind me that he finally notices Gram. I can't see Dad, but Gram raises her hand in greeting and smiles at him. I know Dad will figure out it is me in the booth with Gram because my curly hair is a beacon in the harbor of any room.

I lean across the table and whisper to my grandmother: "What should I do?"

Gram holds my hand. "I don't know, Punkin. Do you want to talk to him?"

I do. I want to put this stupid, senseless feud behind us. For better and worse, this is the man who raised me. Right or wrong, the complicated, stormy man here in this café still owns a piece of my heart. I have made several attempts to reconnect with him throughout the years but am always rebuffed.

Before any decision can be made, the telephone next to the counter rings. I know before the waitress picks it up that it will be for my dad.

"Bobby . . . telephone's for you . . . " She balances the receiver on top of the wall phone and picks up a plate of pancakes.

My dad brushes by the waitress on the way to the phone and comes within inches of our booth, his back to me. He grabs the phone and we hear his side of the conversation.

"Yeah, I can do that. I'll be there in a few minutes."

Dad hangs up the phone and shouts to the waitress. "Cancel my order, honey, I've got to run."

Dad turns toward me and sucker-punches me with a bruising glare, and then turns on his heel and walks out the door without a word. I am crushed and angry. Part of me wants to run after him, throw myself at his feet and beg him: "Please talk to me . . . let's work through this . . . you're my dad." Another part of me thinks: *Screw him. It's his loss. I don't need this shit.*

Grandma reaches over and covers my trembling hand with hers. I can't meet her eyes. I stroke Gram's perfectly manicured hand, soft and worn with age spots, and say a prayer of thanks that she is here with me.

A month later, my dad is dead.

• • •

Dad is 59 years old when he dies on August 31, 2001—10 years to the day after my grandfather's death. We hadn't spoken one word to each other in those ten long years.

I'm home in Nashville, at lunch with friends, when my cell phone rings with my brother Rick's name on the caller ID. I ignore the call. He calls again a few minutes later. I excuse myself and walk outside to answer the phone.

"Sissy, Dad passed away this morning. He had a heart attack and died instantly."

The traffic noise from the triangle of Broadway, Division and West End intrudes as I struggle to hear my brother and absorb his words. I'm engulfed in the August heat, my sandal-covered feet sweat above the hot asphalt of the parking lot and my sundress sticks to my legs.

It cannot end this way, I think. We have too much unfinished business, Dad and I. Too much that needs to be said. It can't end like this. It can't. As much as I hate him, I love him. As much anger as there is between us, I feel tenderness. As much as I don't under-stand about my dad, I understand completely. He'll never know this now.

"Should I come home?" I ask Rick.

"Yes," he replies. "Mom says to come home."

It may seem like a strange question to ask, but I know from the family grapevine that Dad has instructed friends to bar me from his funeral. He didn't want me in his life and he didn't want me in death, either.

As I drive home to pack a suitcase, I try to console myself with facts. Dad's had a bad heart for more than 20 years. I'm surprised he's lasted this long. He died quickly and painlessly, up north, in the place he loved most, with my mom at his side, the woman he'd loved for more than 40 years, the woman he married knowing she was pregnant with me, another man's child.

Once home, I call Jennifer, who is now 21. She moved to Maine four months earlier with her boyfriend and is six months pregnant with her first child. I know this news will devastate her. Dad is her darling Grandpa, a man she has loved without question or reservation no matter the history between him and me. There is no easy way to tell my daughter that her grandpa is dead. I try to soothe her, tell her I love her, that Grandpa will always love her. Jenny lets loose with a guttural moan of unbridled grief. It takes thirty minutes to calm her enough to help her make travel arrange-ments for the funeral.

I am in agony all night. I want to cry—I try to cry—but the tears are unwilling. I remember the last time I saw Dad and the with-ering look he gave me before he walked out of the café. I should have gone after him, I think. Now it's too late. It will always be too late.

The early memories of us as father and daughter wash in like a strong tide, and then recede gradually—slow enough that I choke on the bittersweet waves like too much saltwater in my throat.

The next day, I drive up Interstate 65 with a bag full of CDs. I listen to upbeat music and am determined to stay strong if only for Jenny. I'm nervous about my mom. Although we had exchanged a few emails in recent years, we haven't spent any time together in the last decade. She was so dependent on Dad, so close to him, their intimacy always a puzzle but equally rock solid.

I pick Jennifer up at Chicago O'Hare airport and we arrive in Milwaukee by late afternoon. I haven't set foot in my mother's house in ten years. Everything has changed. The suede earth-toned 70s era furniture exchanged for overstuffed couches and chairs in light pastel fabric. Apparently Mom is a fan of Thomas Kinkade and several of his large paintings hang in the living room. The brown shag carpeting is gone, replaced by an off-white low-pile synthetic.

Jenny kicks her shoes off, drops her bag and flings herself into my mother's arms. She and her grandmother have a special bond. I feel awkward as I watch this display, and even more so when Jenny makes the rounds to hug and kiss my brothers. They are all happy to see each other, to be together in this time of grief. I've never fit in with this family.

Rick, perhaps sensing my discomfort, walks over to hug me. He's about to walk out the door to go to the funeral home. I decide to go with him, more to get out of the house than anything.

The funeral home is quiet when we arrive. Dad's body is prepared for the wake. The funeral director leads us into a large, wood-paneled stateroom. I hold on to Rick's arm as we approach the open casket. My heartbeat and Dad's death are omnipresent in the room. The stillness vibrates between us. I'm sure I must be walking, but it feels like I'm floating toward him.

Dad lies in a crushed velvet casket and wears a suit I don't recognize. He looks empty yet more at peace than the man I once knew. Standing over him is too much. I lose complete control of my emotions. I throw the upper half of my body on top of him, cling to his mannequin-like body and wail: "Daddy, Daddy, Daddy . . . " Rick gently pulls me away from the coffin. We hold each other and cry.

• • •

I return to Nashville on September 9, 2001, after helping Mom deal with the details of Dad's sudden death. When the planes hit the World Trade Center on September 11, my grief plummets like an elevator in free fall.

If I wasn't quite battered enough in one week, Karl, my boyfriend of six years now, dumps me unceremoniously and takes up with a woman at his office. Truth be told, Karl isn't much of a boyfriend—there is no real intimacy between us and our relationship is oddly shallow. I have thought about splitting with him often in recent years. Yet, maybe because of his inconsiderate timing, the break-up is hard on me nonetheless.

The week after September 11, my friend and co-worker Bill Cody nearly dies of complications from a rare blood disorder. Bill pulls through, but the following month Karl's sister Julie dies of cancer and his brother Kurt dies from AIDS within a couple of weeks of each other. During the final weeks of her life, Julie comforted *me* about my break up with her brother. "Don't complain or explain," she writes to me. Her words stay with me to this day. To add insult to injury, Karl takes his new girlfriend to California for Julie's funeral while I am left behind to deal with the loss on my own.

Once again, I turn to Patrick Dean for guidance to help me through my grief. Over a long-distance phone call Patrick reminds me that each day is a gift, and we don't know whether or not we'll have another. "Any day out of a hospital is a good day," he repeats his favorite line. Patrick suggests I put my grief into a closet that I visit at the end of each day. So I do. Each morning I get up, exercise, eat breakfast, go to work and go through the motions of having a life. I give myself permission to crawl into bed every night at 9:00, and once I am in bed I can visit my grief closet and cry and wail and feel sorry for myself until the next morning.

The lessons from Patrick return to me slowly, like the sweetness of an old lover. By the end of 2001, I don't have room in my life for anger, fear, envy or resentment, and I refuse to let that poison seep into my psyche. Instead I focus on what I do want. I open myself up to new experiences and meet extraordinary people, including Paul Whitfield.

When I meet Paul, I am the operations manager at Great American Country (GAC) cable network, where I produce a live, call-in, video-request show called CRL and a classic country music program hosted by Bill Cody. We run our shows out of Reba McEntire's Starstruck Studios on Music Row. Paul built the broadcast studio at Starstruck, and he often comes in to repair and upgrade the equipment. One day, Paul is standing on a ladder as I hand him gels for the set lights. We talk about music and art and Paul says: "I hate to see society decompose into abject mediocrity." Smarts and heart in one statement. He has my attention from that moment forward.

After all the years of looking for love, Paul is my big score. His deep thinking is just one of the reasons I fall for him. Paul is a grown-up with the playfulness of a child. He doesn't try to fit in or impress anyone. He is a complete individual, yet he's comfortable to be around. Paul is open, affectionate, a good listener with a wry sense of humor and the most soulful eyes I've ever looked into. And his lips. I can stare at them all day and never get tired of looking at Paul's lips. His long, black hair hangs down to the middle of his back. There aren't many men who can pull off this look, but Paul on a ladder in tight jeans with his hair in a ponytail is pure sex appeal.

Our first date for late morning coffee lasts more than four hours. I excuse myself twice and huddle in the hallway next to the rest room to whisper in my cell phone and cancel my other meetings for the day. My attraction to Paul is so strong I cannot pull myself away from him.

Again, we talk about music. I tell Paul about my love for Joe Ely and the Flatlanders. Paul says it reminds him of the 1884 satirical novella *Flatland*, a story about a fictional two-dimensional world, which observes the hierarchy of Victorian culture. This leads us to a discussion about collective consciousness and how after 9/11, the entire world believed we were all in this together. Now the public debate is more focused on destroying the enemy than any real problem solving.

Paul and I agree that instead of social justice, our society is now driven by ubiquitous self-interest with no regard for the greater good, and people clutch their beliefs with a white-knuckled vigor that leaves no room for compromise.

Heavy stuff for a first date, yet I am impressed, even turned on, that I am dealing with an intelligent, thoughtful, sexy man who treats me as an intellectual equal. Our relationship unfolds slowly (yet oh, so sweetly) because Paul works on the touring side of the business and is on the road with Kenny Chesney as a video engineer.

Meanwhile, I get myself into a jam at work for arguing about democracy with Charlie Daniels. Yes, that Charlie Daniels—the long-haired country boy, Devil-went-down-to-Georgia, 70s pot-smoking hippie turned right-wing conservative Christian. After 9/11, American emotions are up and down like teenage hormones. Right, left, Republican, Democrat, Christian, non-Christian—

suddenly everyone's opinions take on a new fury. We're on the verge of war, damn it. You're either with us or against us. You're a good American or a traitor. There is nothing between.

I never thought of myself as particularly political. I have my opinions on democracy and I've voted in every election since I became of age in 1979. But, I'm neither a chest-thumping, FOX-watching conservative nor (in the words of Todd Snider) "a pot-smoking, porn-watching, lazy-ass hippie."

My trouble at work begins when I get an email from Charlie Daniels forwarded by a publicist. The email is Daniels's "Open Letter to the Hollywood Bunch," and in it he takes the actor Sean Penn to task for traveling to Iraq: "Sean Penn, you're a traitor to the United States of America. You gave aid and comfort to the enemy. How many American lives will your little 'fact-finding trip' to Iraq cost?"

The first time I receive the email, I delete it. The second time I get the same email, I write back and ask to be taken off the mailing list. The third time, I respond and write that that civil discourse is the cornerstone of democracy. Americans' freedom of speech is protected by the First Amendment. Just like Charlie Daniels is free to say whatever he wants, so is the Hollywood Bunch.

GAC is not happy that I responded and they fire me. My termination is debated publicly and in the media, but I am lucky. Although I receive hateful emails from several people on Music Row who are more than happy to tell me my career in country music is over, I am blown away by the number of songwriters, artists, and music industry colleagues who come to my defense. John McEuen from the Nitty Gritty Dirt Band calls me from Los Angeles to tell me that he asked GAC to pull all the Dirt Band videos from their library. I run into Rodney Crowell, who grabs me in a bear hug and says: "We've got your back." Radney Foster calls me and says: "I have my checkbook out, how much do you need?" Beth Nielsen Chapman calls the First Amendment Center to ask if they can do anything to help me. Phone calls and emails pour in from all over the country. I am deeply moved by the support of the music community. Thankfully, the attention on me doesn't last long. Less than a week after I'm fired from GAC, Natalie Maines of the Dixie Chicks creates a firestorm when she states from a London stage that she is embarrassed that President George W. Bush is a Texan. To this day, my heart aches for Natalie, Emily and Martie. A couple of years before this event, Music Row hailed the Dixie Chicks for saving the country music format. Now several country radio stations hold steamroller parties to crush Dixie Chicks CDs. Despicable.

While I try to figure out my next move, Paul begins a job with Bruce Springsteen as the video engineer-in-charge for Springsteen's *The Rising* tour and heads to Europe. He has some time off in Italy and, since I am unemployed, I join Paul for a romantic week in Firenze. While I am in Italy falling in love with Paul, my friend Al Bunetta at Oh Boy Records talks about me with songwriting legend Kris Kristofferson and Al hires me to help with publicity on Kris's new record.

In my first conversation with Kris the day after I return from Europe, he says: "I like that you stood up for your beliefs even though it cost you your job." Kris and I hit it off from the beginning. I meet Kris and Lisa for the first time in Chicago at the WTTW television studio for a taping of the music show *Soundstage*. Actor Russell Crowe and his band Thirty Odd Foot of Grunts open the show and Russell joins Kris on a few songs for Kris's closing set. During the downtime, Kris, Lisa and I get a chance to talk and it feels like I've known them my entire life. We click immediately.

I leave Chicago with pages of notes and start to build my public relations plan for the release of Kris's *Live From San Francisco* CD. I throw myself into my work with Kris, which is a dream job. My personal life is great, too. Paul and I have grown from dating to a solidly committed relationship, and life with him is beyond anything my girlish romantic notions could have imagined. Paul is sweeter and more loving than any man I've known since my grandfather. I am happier than I've ever been. I fool myself into believing that I am over my dad's death.

With the love of my life, Paul Whitfield, in 2003.

CHAPTER 16

Please Remember Me

I get my wake up call early morning on Friday, September 12, 2003. The ringing telephone startles me from a sound sleep and my heart thumps hard as I check the clock on my bedside table. Time: 6:35 a.m. I punch my pillow and pull the down comforter over my head. The phone drowns out and goes to voice mail on the third ring. I'm almost asleep again when it rings a second time. My consciousness drifts to Paul, who's on the east coast with Springsteen, and my family in New England and Wisconsin. When there is bad news I get it from the phone.

I toss the comforter aside and quickly adjust my rumpled pajama bottoms and tank top as I walk out the bedroom door and down the short hall to the den. I grab the cordless phone from its dock and settle into the black leather loveseat. My cat Gabe crawls into my lap, and I pet his soft gray head absently with one hand as I use the other to scroll through Caller ID. *Associated Press. The New York Times*, Clear Channel Radio. Yeah, there's bad news for sure, but at least it's not about my family.

Gabe slides gracefully from my lap and we both walk toward the screen porch. I open the French door to let him out. Birds sing as they fly from tree to tree on a warm, sunny morning in Nashville, a soft breeze wafting through the screens, fluttering the wood chimes. I breathe the humid air deeply and brace myself.

I play the first message: "Hi Tamara, this is John Gerome from AP. I'd like to get an interview with Kris Kristofferson about the death of Johnny Cash. Please call me back."

The phone tumbles from my hand and skitters across the wooden deck. I sink into the patio chair. Johnny Cash. Johnny Cash is dead. It seems impossible.

I take a few minutes to whisper a mantra: "I'm okay, I'm okay. I can handle this." I listen to the other messages—all requesting interviews with Kris—and flip the radio to WSM-AM. The disc jockey confirms the news. Johnny Cash died early this morning at Baptist Hospital in Nashville.

I walk back into the kitchen and dial the AP reporter's number. "John, Tamara Saviano. Yeah, I just heard. I haven't talked to Kris yet. He's in Hawaii and it's the middle of the night there. Give me a few hours and I'll try to get you on the phone with him later this morning."

The other line beeps and I hear my cell phone ring off in the distance. I'm in for a long day.

Kris and Johnny were like brothers, and I've heard Kris tell the story of his first meeting with Cash many times. It was Kris's first visit to Nashville. On leave from the Army and hanging out at the Grand Ole Opry with Cowboy Jack Clement, Kris watched Johnny from backstage. "I thought he was the most exciting performer I'd ever seen," Kris always says. "John was skinny as a snake and prowled the stage like a panther looking like he might explode. He shook my hand and it was electric."

Their friendship developed when Kris moved to Nashville to be a songwriter. He worked as a janitor at Columbia studios and met Cash during a recording session. Cash loved his songs. He recorded Kris's song "Sunday Morning Coming Down," invited Kris to perform with him at Newport Folk Festival and had Kris as a guest on his TV program, *The Johnny Cash Show*. Over the years the friendship deepened to one of mutual respect, admiration and brotherhood. In the 1980s, Kris and Cash traveled the world together with Waylon Jennings and Willie Nelson as The Highwaymen, a country music supergroup. Kris and John have been friends for nearly 40 years. And now Cash is dead.

As I process everything, I let the phone ring. Voice mail catches calls as I put the teakettle. I need a few more minutes to pull myself together before calling Kris. Johnny Cash songs run through my mind and I think about my dad. I'm shaking.

I know what I have to do, but the phone feels too heavy for my hand. I weakly punch the Kristoffersons' home number in Hawaii. Lisa answers on the first ring.

"Lisa, it's Tamara. I'm sorry to call so early." I pause—an attempt to control the waver in my voice. "You've heard about Johnny Cash?"

"Yes," Lisa replies. "We've been up all night." She sounds as if she's been crying.

"I'm so sorry." The words are syrup in my mouth. "How's Kris?" I hear him in the background asking who is on the phone.

Lisa breaks away from me to answer Kris. "It's Tamara. Here, talk to her."

"Kris, I'm sorry. I'm so sorry for your loss."

"Thanks, Tamara." His grief is palpable.

"Listen, I hate to bother you with this, but the phone is ringing off the hook with press requests. Do you want me to put out a statement? Do you want to do any interviews?"

Kris clears his throat. I hate this. One of Kris' dearest friends died a few hours ago and instead of having time with his family to

grieve, I'm asking him to talk to strangers who can't possibly understand the depth of his relationship with Cash.

Kris, gracious as always, finally answers. "Yeah, I'll do some
interviews. It might do me good to talk about John."

Lisa comes back to the phone, and we block out several hours
that afternoon and over the weekend for Kris to take calls.

"I'll email you a list in a couple of hours," I say.

"Okay," Lisa replies. "We'll be in Nashville on Sunday. I'll keep
you posted on funeral arrangements."

"Take care of each other," I say before hanging up.

I spend a tedious, yet emotional day answering two phones,
fielding email requests and coordinating interview times. Dad is
right there with me, taunting and jabbing and smirking. I can hear
his voice clearly: "Who did you sleep with to get this job?"

The busywork keeps me from falling apart. Kris does interviews
with many media outlets including *People, Rolling Stone, The Ten-
nessean, Entertainment Weekly, Associated Press, Reuters, Billboard,
Time, Newsweek, The Washington Post*, CBS, CNN, CMT, and too
many radio stations to count. The frenzy stops around 11 p.m.,
nearly 17 hours after it started. I schedule more interviews for the
next day, but we have a brief overnight reprieve. I pray for rest but
Dad is omnipresent and—just like always—he refuses to be shut
down.

• • •

Johnny Cash's music is all over radio and television in the days
after his death, and everything I hear brings back a piece of my dad.
He continues to haunt me even months and years after Cash's
funeral. His spirit drifts around me much like his music filled my
childhood. I find myself bringing up his name, telling stories about

him, and I even grudgingly admit that he was once a crucial part of my life—that he shaped me as much or maybe even more than anyone or anything else had.

I long to remember the good parts during my childhood. As part of this yearning, I return to Mapleview to reconnect with my friends and reclaim my roots. An eagle flies above and accompanies me down the picturesque stretch of Church Road in Conover. Patty Loveless is on the radio singing "How Can I Help You Say Goodbye" as I turn onto McPeak Road. Tears warm my face and neck and yet surprisingly I feel at peace.

My homecoming sparks conversations about Dad, and each of my Mapleview pals tells me how much Dad changed for the better in the decade we didn't speak. After Bob and Dorothy Lee's son Ryan was killed in a car accident, it was my dad who kept Ryan's memorial place on the highway cleared of brush and mowed. When Bob Lee was battling cancer, Dad drove him to chemo treatments, helped Dorothy around the house and pulled the dock out of the water for the winter. According to Dorothy, Dad also read Bible passages and hung a Christian fish symbol on his garage door. The burning question is: If he changed so much for the better, why did he still rebuff me?

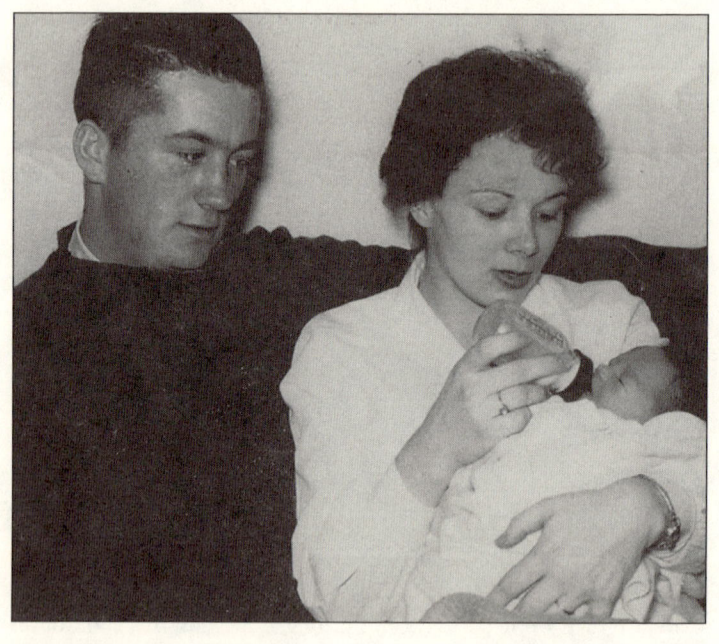

Dad, Mom and me shortly after my birth in February 1961.

CHAPTER 17

Try a Little Tenderness

Dad lingers in the back of my mind, but life in Nashville is great. I'm president of the Americana Music Association board and am the producer for the annual Americana Honors & Awards show at Nashville's Ryman Auditorium. During a short lunch break on Awards-show day, my friend Grant Alden and I run across the alley from our base at the Ryman. We stand in line at Jack's Barbecue for our pork sandwiches, baked beans, corn bread and fried apples. Grant grabs a scarred wood table by the window. I take a seat and immediately begin squirting Tennessee mild sauce on my shredded pig.

As I lick sauce off my thumb, I tell Grant about my recent trip home to Wisconsin. Paul and I recently moved in together, and we used money from his house sale to invest in a home on Lake Michigan just six blocks from Grandma Jeanne. Now my mom and her sisters have decided to retire to Arizona, taking Gram with them. I'm annoyed. "The only reason we bought the house is so I could go home and spend more time with my family," I complain.

Grant is never one to mince words. "I think there is something in Wisconsin that has a hold on you," he says. "Maybe you should figure out what it is."

. . .

I started with my mother. Mom always says the past doesn't matter. It is difficult for her to talk about my childhood and the problems that led to our estrangement. To encourage Mom to open up, I made a CD mix of some of Dad's favorite songs: Johnny Cash's "Folsom Prison Blues," "Orange Blossom Special," "Daddy Sang Bass," and "Jackson." Otis Redding's "Fa-Fa-Fa-Fa-Fa (Sad Song)," "Sittin' On the Dock of the Bay," and "Try a Little Tenderness." "Kiss an Angel Good Morning" (Charley Pride), "Respect" (Aretha Franklin), "Sweet Soul Music" (Arthur Conley), "In the Midnight Hour" (Wilson Pickett), "Brown Eyed Handsome Man" (Johnny Rivers) and "Get Ready" (Rare Earth). And, of course, Charlie Rich's "The Most Beautiful Girl," "Behind Closed Doors," and "Nothin' in the World (To Do With Me)."

Mom picked me up at Sky Harbor International Airport in Phoenix. It's a 30-minute drive from the airport to Mom's place in Apache Junction. I slipped the CD into her player and she smiled and laughed, immediately recognizing the opening of "Brown Eyed Handsome Man."

"I haven't heard this song in years!"

"I thought you might like to hear some of Dad's old songs," I said.

Mom looked at me knowingly, but to my surprise, she went with the moment. As we listened to the CD heading east through Tempe and Mesa, Mom talked easily about Dad. We played the "Remember when?" game throughout the drive. Occasionally, Mom would turn a song up and laugh to herself, lost in her own memories.

When we arrived at her house, I wasted no time in throwing my suitcase in the guest room and grabbed my tape recorder. Mom had poured herself a cup of coffee and sat at the table in her spacious screen porch. She rolled her eyes at the recorder but didn't object when I turned it on. Over the next four hours, Mom spilled everything.

In 1952, my mother, Sandra Leavitt, was a well-mannered 11-year-old from a respectable middle-class family with community ties stretching back more than a hundred years. Mom and her five sisters lived an idyllic life with my grandparents and great-grandparents in an old-fashioned bungalow in Cudahy. They lived just six blocks west of Lake Michigan on a wide street with newly minted cement sidewalks framed by grand oak and maple trees.

Mom told me she met Bob Ruditys when he was 10 years old one winter day at the ice skating pond in Sheridan Park, an event I have imagined many times. Mom's long braided pigtails stick out of her hat and sail behind her as she skated. Her movements were restrained by bulky winter clothing, the pants and long underwear, winter coat and woolen mittens. (I'm sure my grandma bundled Mom tight before letting her out of the house.) Dad, on the other hand, flies around the rink in a threadbare coat over a flannel shirt with no long johns under his dungarees, no hat on his head, no parental concern about how he was dressed on this cold day.

I can picture them meeting for the first time on the ice that day, Dad easily smitten with Mom's fresh-scrubbed beauty, demure smile and corny sense of humor. For her part, I see Mom flirting with Dad, her heart spinning like a pinwheel. She thought he was cute, charming and maybe just a little dark and dangerous. It's not off the mark to imagine Dad as a lonely boy hiding his sadness behind a phony swagger and a group of rabble-rouser friends—characteristics that followed him to adulthood. My mom—even at age 11—saw right through the bad boy image to the tenderness buried underneath his arrogance. Perhaps because she glimpsed his heart, there was an instant connection between my mom and dad—that mysterious infatuation between a boy and girl that isn't easily explained.

Dad walked Mom home from the ice rink that day. I envision them strolling the six blocks up Armour Avenue, a path I have walked myself many times, under a canopy of maple trees past tidy yards settled with the clean and modest bungalows, cottages and flats that shape the working-class neighborhood. The Cudahy town slogan is "Generations of Pride," and they come by it honestly.

After seeing Mom home, Dad continued his walk over the railroad tracks to St. Francis and the house on Nicholson Avenue where he lived with his neglectful alcoholic parents and three older siblings. Dad's home was the antithesis of Sandra's warm and loving family.

During their childhood years, Mom explained their casual acquaintance deepened into a strong friendship. But it was a friendship she had to hide from her parents.

"I was crazy about Bob for years," Mom told me. "And Grandma had always said, 'What do you see in Bob Ruditys?' Around the time of my high school graduation, he showed up drunk one night after a bachelor party. Grandma and Grandpa had company. He came over and he pulled up with his front tire on the curb, and Grandpa's car was right in front of him. I walked around the other side of the car, and he was so drunk. I told Bob, 'Just get out of here. Go home.' He puts the car into gear and hits Grandpa's car. And Grandma comes out on the porch and she yells at me, 'Get out of the street! Get out of the street! He's going to kill you!' It's funny now, but it sure wasn't then."

Although they secretly carried a torch for each other throughout their teen years, Mom and Dad weren't romantic until it was thrust upon them by unimaginable circumstances.

In 1959, my mom graduated from Cudahy High School while Dad was still a student at Boy's Tech. After high school, Mom landed a job working a morning and evening split shift as a tele-phone operator for Wisconsin Bell. During her afternoons off, Mom and her co-worker friends walked around downtown Mil-waukee taking in the scene of sailors on break from Chicago's Great Lakes naval base.

"Milwaukee was just loaded with sailors in their uniforms," Mom recalled. "They came up for the weekends from the naval base and would hang out on Wisconsin Avenue looking for girls. I needed a date for a party at my friend Sally's house so somebody said, 'Okay, let's go shopping for your guy.' We were waiting for a light on the corner of Third and Wisconsin, and I glanced across the street and saw this cute sailor. We locked eyes. I said 'I'll take that one over there.' He came to the party with me and after that we were together every weekend."

Mom didn't see Bob Ruditys during the spring and summer of 1960, and dated Mike Saviano. She was wrapped up in her life work-ing at Wisconsin Bell, hanging out with her girlfriends and seeing Mike on the weekends.

Mom knew she was pregnant by August. In 1960 this was the worst thing that could happen to a girl. Mom worried about the dis-grace to her family and how the pregnancy would change her life. Mom called Mike at the naval base to break the news to him.

Mike panicked. "Oh, my God. What are we going to do? My parents are going to kill me."

"You don't understand how upsetting it was to be pregnant and not married in those days," Mom said. "The disgrace was over-whelming to me."

On the bus ride home from work the next day, Mom, fright-ened and dejected, spotted Bob Ruditys on the sidewalk with his friends. Impulsively, she pulled the bell and the driver let her off at the next stop.

"I saw Bob," she said, "and the thought went through my head that maybe he knew somebody that would help me get an abortion."

Mom cried when she told me this. It must be incredibly difficult to tell your daughter that you wanted to abort her, but I got it. It was 1960. Abortion was not safe and legal like it is now. I imagine there are women all over America who were forced to have children they didn't want.

Mom asked Bob to help find an abortionist.

"I will not help you find a doctor," Bob said adamantly. "We'll get married. I'll marry you."

Mom was touched by Bob's chivalrous offer and held back her tears. She couldn't accept. Bob was not the father of this baby and, scared as she was, Mom didn't believe it was the right thing to do. She confessed to Bob that she and Mike had a date Friday to discuss her condition.

Mom was drained by the time Friday rolled around. Her nights had been sleepless. She finished her shift that afternoon and stepped onto the sidewalk outside Wisconsin Bell. She gazed up at the bright August sun, deeply inhaled the fresh Lake Michigan breeze and blocked the sun with her hand. Mom looked down the street and saw Mike, wearing his Navy uniform, walking toward her. Bob abruptly pulled his car to the curb before Mom could even raise her hand to wave at Mike. Bob leaned over and opened the passenger door. They stared at each other for a moment. Then Bob spoke: "Make up your mind right now, him or me."

Mom hesitated. Facts flashed before her eyes: She's only known Mike for a few months. He's in the Navy. He'll be shipped out eventually. His family lives in Boston, an incredible distance from Milwaukee to a girl who doesn't travel far from home. Go with Mike and Mom certainly would be left alone with this baby. She made the split-second decision and jumped into the car with Bob. Mom didn't look back at Mike approaching as Bob drove toward the safety of the suburban life they had always known.

Paul and me on the Grammy red carpet February 13, 1995.

CHAPTER 18

To Live Is to Fly

I truly began to make peace with Mom after the interview with her. Her astonishing disclosure changed my perception of my parents, and it took months for me to digest her confession. Unfortunately, by this time, it was too late for me to make amends with my dad.

Maybe because I confronted the demon rather than running and hiding, I managed to let go of the hostility between Dad and me. Bob Ruditys is gone. Letting go granted me the freedom I've craved for my entire life. In my middle age, I see Dad with clear eyes. I now have the judgment to look at my dad's life holistically—to consider his childhood, his issues and his pain.

I suppose this book is my way of making peace with Dad. There was plenty of pain in our home, yet underneath my dad's anguish, love and joy struggled for release and sometimes managed to burst forward like a sprinter on his last gasp to the finish line.

While considering writing this book and in an effort to recapture my earliest memories, I begin to collect Dad's favorite music. From this vantage point, and considering my dad's bigotry, I find it ironic that he was drawn to music that arose from the black experience, civil rights and the South. Along with Cash, the Staple Singers,

Sam Cooke, Otis Redding and Wilson Pickett created the foundation of my dad's record collection.

I made my own pilgrimage to Memphis in a quest to learn as much as I could about the history of Stax and Sun Records. At the Stax Museum, Dad's ghost looks over my shoulder as I examine the eerie paper trail that tells the story of Otis Redding's death: a car rental contract; aviation receipts; a hotel bill; the death certificate and logbook of sympathy calls; and condolence telegrams from the Staple Singers, Booker T. and the MGs, the Temptations and others. All of the items seem a tangible link to my dad.

Otis died in the frigid waters of Lake Monona in Madison, Wisconsin, after his plane crashed there on a foggy day in December of 1967. Ninety miles away, Otis's early LPs, including *Complete & Unbelievable: The Otis Redding Dictionary of Soul*, are fixtures on Dad's turntable. "Fa-Fa-Fa-Fa-Fa (Sad Song)" and "Try a Little Tenderness" are regular (and many times unwanted) lullabies for my brothers and me.

It's extraordinary that the common thread of music that embodies Dad, Johnny Cash, Otis Redding, my past and present, beckons me to this place at this time. As I listen to old country, folk and soul CDs, the music awakens my creativity. My imagination begins to percolate like a bubbling hot tub, and I feel alive with wonder and possibility.

It's during this time of reflection that I start a nonprofit arts organization called American Roots Publishing. I think about our old mission statement from Sundance Broadcasting: The Most Fun Wins. That's the kind of company I intend to build. For our first project, I partner with my friends David Macias and Steve Fishell to produce a tribute album to Stephen Foster titled *Beautiful Dreamer: The Songs of Stephen Foster*.

Mavis Staples comes to Nashville to record "Hard Times Come

Again No More" for the collection. I pick Mavis and her sister Yvonne up at the Nashville airport. Mavis greets me as if we are old friends and upon her first bear hug, I am certain we've been spiritually connected from my childhood. That day in the studio, I smile so much my cheeks ache for days after. The afternoon with Mavis is an incredible experience itself, but the occasion is heightened by memories of Dad as he dances through the house and sings "Respect Yourself."

· · ·

On February 13, 2005, I am at the Grammy Awards as a nominee for producing *Beautiful Dreamer: The Songs of Stephen Foster*. The whole scene is dreamlike. Paul holds my hand as we sit next to each other on metal folding chairs at the pre-telecast in a big boxy room at the Staples Center in Los Angeles. My co-producers sit a few chairs down the row.

I'm nervous even though I don't believe we are going to win. We've got stiff competition with wonderful projects by Beausoleil, Norman & Nancy Blake, Rosalie Sorrels and Dave Van Ronk. As we watch each winner take the stage, I become more agitated. I pick at the delicate rhinestones on my vintage emerald green gown, which I bought on eBay for a hundred bucks.

Dad is with me. I see him in his tight, white T-shirt and black pants—his belt buckle undone and hanging down. He shimmies around the kitchen, glass of brandy in hand, to Tony Joe White's "Polk Salad Annie." I can't push the vivid image away. He jerks his head, bites his bottom lip and shakes his body with abandon . . . it's all here in blazing Technicolor when I'm trying to concentrate on the scene before me.

When our category of Best Traditional Folk Album flashes on

the video screen, Paul squeezes my hand. The Christian band Jars of Clay presents the Grammy for this category. They seem to read the list of nominees in unintelligible slow motion as the room pitches forward and the overhead lights blur. Paul puts his arm around me and I snap back into lucidity when I hear our names: "And the Grammy goes to Steve Fishell, David Macias and Tamara Saviano for *Beautiful Dreamer: The Songs of Stephen Foster.*"

Oh. My. God. David and Steve jump up. Paul kisses me. Our friends Tom and Anna cheer and hug us. David drapes his arm around my shoulders to steady me as we walk toward the stage. Our Nashville bunch cheers from the audience, and I catch the eye of a longtime colleague, Fletcher Foster. He pumps his fist in the air and applauds. It lifts me up to see the joy on Fletcher's face. David, Steve and I join hands as we walk up the stairs to accept our Grammy.

David thanks the audience for supporting arts education because our album was created for a nonprofit. Steve thanks all the musicians and others who helped get the project off the ground. When it is my turn to step to the microphone I say: "Stephen Foster died 142 years ago and it's about time he got this." I raise the Grammy high. "This is for Stephen Foster."

I look out into the audience to see my kindred spirits in the music world beam up at us like proud parents. Then I spot Dad's shadow. He looks like he did the day of my high school graduation—young, confident and handsome. He looks around the room and declares to anyone who will listen: "That's my daughter. That's my Penelope." Then he looks directly at me, lifts his voice and sings, "Hey, did you happen to see the most beautiful girl in the world . . . "

As the sound of applause rings around Dad's voice, I grab the hands of my friends and leave the stage.

It's been more than nine years since we won the Grammy for *Beautiful Dreamer: The Songs of Stephen Foster*. At the time, it was the biggest moment of my life. I couldn't have imagined that everything would only get better.

That night at the Grammy after-party, Paul and I were talking with our friend and collaborator Tom Frouge between champagne toasts. We had a quite a dilemma: How in the world would we find a worthy project to follow our now award-winning Stephen Foster tribute? Tom pointed out the obvious—my relationship with Kris Kristofferson. Kris would be 70 years old the next year and we had the perfect opportunity to honor him. So, we did.

The Pilgrim: A Celebration of Kris Kristofferson was released in June 2006. Producing the Stephen Foster tribute was great fun, but honoring Kris, a man I know and love, and sharing the process with him was truly extraordinary. He was deeply touched by the tribute. I remember the tears flowing down Kris's cheeks when he heard Rosanne Cash's recording of "Lovin' Him Was Easier (Than Anything I'll Ever Do Again)." Late one night, he called and asked for Marta Gomez's phone number. He said he was so blown away by her take on "The Circle" that he had to call her immediately.

Kris and I were sitting in an SUV in the California desert on the set of a video shoot for "This Old Road" when I showed him the tribute album's cover art. "Look at that old photograph," Kris said, echoing the lyrics from the song. "Is it really you?" Then he hugged me and said, "Tamara, this is the nicest thing anyone has ever done for me." Whether or not that's true, we shared a moment of unbounded joy that day and we have had many, many more since.

My next project was *The Bluegrass Elvises,* recorded by my friends Shawn Camp and Billy Burnette and released on the thirtieth anniversary of Elvis Presley's death in 2007. Shawn is the biggest Elvis fan I've ever known. Shawn and his then girlfriend Carla, Paul and I went to Memphis together for the weekend that would have been Elvis's seventieth birthday to visit Lauderdale Court, the apartment building where Elvis lived during his childhood. On the same trip, Shawn took us all to Graceland. Talk about fun—Shawn knew more than the tour guide. Then on a media trip with Shawn around the same time, we listened to the Sirius Satellite Radio Elvis channel for three days straight. Let me tell you, living and breathing Elvis Presley with Shawn Camp is unbeatable.

I took a break from producing tribute albums to start writing this memoir in 2008. My best memory that year: Paul and I happily eloped that June. We married at the Lake County courthouse in Waukegan, Illinois—the same place my mom married Bob Ruditys 48 years earlier—while Paul was on break from the European leg of Bruce Springsteen's *Magic* tour.

Now, anyone who knows me knows that Guy Clark is my favorite songwriter. I name-checked him in the liner notes of the Stephen Foster tribute and even Kris has introduced me by saying "This is Tamara. Guy Clark is her favorite songwriter." I worked as the publicist for Guy's 2006 album *Workbench Songs* and again for *Somedays The Song Writes You* in 2009. The following year, I somehow managed to convince Guy to let me write his definitive biography, which is still a work in progress. That book might be the most mind-blowing and wonderful thing I've ever gotten myself into. I've spent the last couple years blissfully traipsing around Texas (sometimes with Guy, sometimes without) tracking down the stories from his amazing life and meeting and talking with his closest friends. Not to mention spending hours upon hours interviewing Guy himself in the storied basement workshop where he writes those incredible songs right here in Nashville. Those are times no money can buy.

I recently put Guy's biography on hold to produce my third tribute album, the most challenging and fulfilling one yet. After two long and wonderful years in the making, we released *This One's For Him: A Tribute to Guy Clark*, a 30-track, double CD set to celebrate Guy's seventieth birthday in 2011. During the week of his birthday, the Center for Texas Music History sponsored the tribute concert "Wish I Was in Austin: A Seventieth Birthday Celebration of Guy Clark" at the Long Center in Austin, Texas. What a night! First, I got to watch artist after artist from our tribute album—from Lyle Lovett and Joe Ely to Jerry Jeff Walker, Rodney Crowell and a dozen others—perform Guy's songs, Then, the absolute thrill of a lifetime: I introduced Guy in front of thousands in a sold-out crowd before he came onstage to play his own set.

This One's For Him: A Tribute to Guy Clark was honored as Americana Album of the year at the 2012 Americana Honors & Awards. And it was nominated for a Grammy for Best Folk Album at the 55th Annual Grammy Awards in February 2013.

I never could have conceived such honors the very first time I picked up Guy's album *Old No. 1* when I was 14 years old. His song "She Ain't Goin' Nowhere" had been the soundtrack to my youth. It had reached for me and rescued me and revived me at all the right times. Giving my acceptance speech at the Americana Awards made me realize how far I'd come. I remembered the young girl who dreamed about being on the gone side of leaving, the girl whose road to happiness seemed endless and impossible and sometimes invisible, the girl who believed throughout it all and with all her heart that there would be a day when she could look back and proudly say: Now, I've gone somewhere.

END

ACKNOWLEDGMENTS

Sometimes it really does take a village. I persevered through researching and writing this memoir with the unconditional love and support of family, friends and colleagues—many who agreed to be my first readers and critics.

My pal Grant Alden encouraged me to start this journey without realizing it over lunch one day in Nashville. His intuition told him I had unfinished business in Wisconsin and I listened to it. Grant, "thank you" doesn't seem enough, but it's all I have.

My business partner and soul sister Alanna Nash acted as my first editor and constant advisor. Without Alanna's faith, I would have given up in the first month. The wonderful author and illustrator Lynda Barry nudged me further down the road with her incomparable "Writing the Unthinkable" workshops. Without Lynda's instruction, I know I never would have put pen to paper. Lynda's assistant Betty Bong (a.k.a. Kelly Hogan) leaped tall buildings to juggle logistics that allowed me to attend the workshops that fit into my schedule. Authors Sheila Bender, Jack Heffron and Meg Files pushed me to the finish line in the Writing It Real workshop they brought to Nashville in 2013. Jack edited the final manuscript and challenged me to dig even deeper. Thank you, Jack.

Julyan Davis painted the gorgeous cover photo and was kind enough to give me permission to use it as the book cover. Bill Lloyd pointed the painting out to me at a gallery event and I fell in love with it. I owe Bill for bringing this painting into my life—the first piece of grown-up art I ever owned.

My client and friend Kris Kristofferson read through this manuscript several times in the middle of an incredibly crazy schedule. In addition to writing the Foreword, Kris and I had several intimate discussions about life and writing and art. Those talks led to new creative adventures and I am ever grateful to Kris for helping me live my dream.

Love and gratitude to my readers and cheerleaders who provided amazing feedback and helped me stay on track: Claire Armbruster, Brian Atkinson, Deb Barnes, Debbie and John Biord, Randy Borland, Carley Brown, Shawn Camp, Stacy Dean Campbell, Marshall Chapman, Pat Compty, Rodney Crowell, Patrick Dean, Val Denn, Leslie DiPiero, Nancy Dutra, Catherine Fleming, Cyndi and Radney Foster, Kim Fowler, Sylvia Giannitrapani, Jen Gunderman, Francine and Gary Hartman, Craig Havighurst, Terri Hendrix, Robert Hicks, Pat Holgate, Taylor Holliday, Norma Horvitz, Lydia Hutchinson, Bob Kayser, Mary Kehoe, Joan Kornblith, Lisa and Kris Kristofferson, Emily and Rob Learned, Ellen Lehman, Dave Marsh, Georgia Middleman, Jeanne Naujeck, Sandy Neese, Kerry O'Neil, Patti and Jerry Osiecki, Gretchen Peters, Rod Picott, Mary Anne Pitt, Ronna Rubin, Rick Ruditys, Mike Saviano, Lauren Sheftell, Sonata Stanton, Michael Streissguth, Catherine Stuart, Corinne Stuart, Jessica Stuart, Michael Stuart, Erika Wollam and Chely Wright.

All the good I am today is due to the influence of my darling grandparents and great-grandparents: My mom's parents Jeanne Laverne Borland Leavitt and Mervin Ellis Leavitt; Grandma Jeanne's parents Myrtle Gertrude Thompson Borland and Oliver Wendall Borland; and Grandpa Ellis's mother, Betsey Caroline Buskerud Leavitt. These five extraordinary individuals held me up and loved me unconditionally. I miss all of them and think about them with love and admiration each day. The Regina Music Box that my great-grandfather Oliver got from his parents as a high school graduation gift in the early 1900s now stands in my own home. It was the first place I discovered recorded music and Stephen Foster. When I put those old discs on, my grandparents are still in the room with me.

I am grateful to my mother, Sandra Joanne Leavitt Ruditys, and my beloved baby brother, Rick Allen Ruditys, for sharing their stories and memories of Dad and allowing me to pursue this book in spite of their uneasiness. My lovely daughter (called Jenny in this book) is infinitely generous to allow me to share part of her story. I love you, Honey.

My mother's former brother-in-law, Larry Rands, graciously shared stories from his friendship with my dad. Our longtime family friend, Bert Treweek, shared memories of his mother (Dad's Godmother) Clara Treweek. Dad's close friend Rudy Konlock mesmerized me with tales from their youth and Corinne Knutson shared stories from her long friendship with my parents. In Ironwood, Michigan, I found my dad's uncle, Tom Wasley—a wealth of information and a kind soul.

Special thanks to my biological father, Mike Saviano, and the Saviano and Stuart families for embracing me as one of your own even though it took more than two decades to find you. I love you. Auntie Corinne, you are like a mother to me. Catherine, you are the sister I always wanted. Uncle Paul, I'm happy to say I am not the captain of the soccer team anymore.

Thank you to Patrick Dean, Dr. Michael Reilly, Dr. Beth Barnett and Dr. Melinda Borthick for physical, psychological and spiritual guidance during the toughest of circumstances.

My dear friend Kay Clary came up with the book title on one of our infamous road trips. The rest of our GNO club—Taylor Holliday, Lisa Jenkins Oltz, Jen Gunderman, Sonata Stanton Rayburn,

Jeanne Naujeck and Catherine Oliva—and my book club—Kathi Whitley, Lisa Shively, Kay Williams, Lynda Miller, Gerrie McDowell and Lydia Hutchinson—provided constant encouragement and laughter during the long and emotional process of writing this memoir.

I am thrilled to have reconnected with my Mapleview family and send a prayer of gratitude and love to Mary Molter Kehoe, Jerry Osiecki Jr. and Patti Nixon Osiecki, Bob Kayser, Dave Murray, Mike Mudler, Kathy Lee and Dorothy Lee. In addition, Mary was my rock during the emotionally charged research trip in Ironwood. Sharing it with her made the trip truly special. Old friends, they shine like diamonds . . .

My childhood schoolmates helped me piece together our lives in St. Francis. This collective memory includes: Monica Brauner, Lori Brockman, Pete Caruso, Jeanne Casper, John Chavez, Louis Conti, Scott Mahuta, Tom McKeon, Matteo Norante, Rob Obradovich, Kathy O'Leary, Daniel Plevak, Tony Plevak, Diane Plonka, Julianne Rosploch, Julie Simon, Chuck Smith and Kay Steinegger.

My professional experience at Sundance Broadcasting laid the groundwork for this wonderful life I've built in Nashville. I will always share the magical bond of the Sundance years with those colleagues—especially mentors Brian Ongaro, Kerry Wolfe, Jerry Arndt, Mitch Morgan and my dear, dear girlfriends Angela Parker and LaVonne Beecher. As the late Mike Jorgenson wrote to me after I won the Grammy: "Once a Sundancer, always a Sundancer."

Above all, I am grateful for my darling husband, Paul Whitfield, the man who puts up with my never-ending changes and neuroses with grace and humor. On top of that, he rarely comments about my uniform of flannel pajamas and a ponytail. I am loved by my Paul and I love him back with all my heart.

Conley (ABKCO Music/Irving Music). Recorded by Arthur Conley.

"Me and Bobby McGee," written by Kris Kristofferson and Fred Foster (Combine Music Corp). Recorded by Janis Joplin.

"Folsom Prison Blues," written by Johnny Cash (Bug Music/House of Cash).

"For the Good Times," written by Kris Kristofferson (Universal Music/Careers). Recorded by Ray Price.

"Ring of Fire," written by Merle Kilgore and June Carter Cash (Painted Desert Music). Recorded by Johnny Cash.

"My Life," written by Billy Joel (Almo Music). Recorded by Billy Joel.

"Evergreen (Love Theme from *A Star Is Born*)," written by Barbra Streisand and Paul Williams (Universal). Recorded by Barbra Streisand.

"Little Girl Lost," written by Kris Kristofferson (Combine Music Corp). Recorded by Kris Kristofferson.

"Only Time Will Tell," written by John Wetton and Geoffrey Downes (Warner Bros. Music Group/BMG). Recorded by Asia.